Consultation

A Universal Lamp of Guidance

D0785180

JOHN E. KOLSTOE

GEORGE RONALD

OXFORD

GEORGE RONALD, Publisher
46 High Street, Kidlington, Oxford, OX5 2DN

Third Reprint 1990

ISBN 0-85398-186-8(Hardcover)
ISBN 0-85398-187-6(Softcover)

Typeset by Sunrise Setting
Torquay, Devon
Printed in England

Contents

	Introduction	1
1	Take Ye Counsel Together	5
	The Lamp of Guidance	6
	The Nature of Bahá'í Consultation	8
	The Bedrock of the World Order	10
2	How to Consult	14
	The Prime Requisites	15
	The Two Conditions	19
	Procedures	22
3	Making Decisions	25
	Collective Decision	25
	Who Makes the Final Decision?	33
4	Improving Consultation	36
	Necessary Skills	36
	Points to Remember	39
	Summary	42
5	Spiritual Assemblies	44
	Spirit	44
	Form	46
	Leadership	47
	Functions of Officers	52
	Practical Considerations	56
	Paper Assemblies	61
	When Decisions are Wrong	62

6   Other Institutions   68
    Institution of the 'Learned'   68
    The Family   70
    The Nineteen Day Feast   73
    The Fund   78
    Summer Schools   79
    Conventions   80

7   Weaving the Social Fabric   81
    Deepening   82
    Teaching   83
    Informal Settings   86
    Business and Professional Affairs   88
    The Non-Bahá'í World   92

8   Individual Differences and Consultation   94
    The True Self   95
    Physical, Emotional and Spiritual Needs   103
    Perceptions   106
    Credibility   109

9   The Search for Truth   112
    Understanding, Real and Imagined   112
    Understanding from Consultation   118
    Four Methods of Comprehension   120
    Illuminating the Search   123
    Unity in Diversity   125

10 Spiritual Battles   127
    Tests and Difficulties   127
    Sources of Tests   129
    Stress   130
    Searching for Solutions   132

11 Challenges to Unity   145
    Common Annoyances   146
    Enduring Inefficiency   149

Attitudes toward Success   153
Conflicting Feelings   159

12 Serious Disturbances   161
    Emotional Problems   161
    Confrontations   162
    Lying   164
    Contentiousness   165
    Jealousy and the Quest for Leadership   169
    Covenant-breaking   172

13 Creating a Healing   173
    Attitudes   175
    Actions   180
    Complete and Enduring Unity   182

14 Reflections on Consultation   186
    Ebb and Flow   186
    Consultation and the Formative Age   188
    The Legacy   190

    Epilogue   192

    Key to References   196

Eugene, a Tlinget Indian of noble lineage, was the first of his people to become a Bahá'í. He has served on the National Spiritual Assembly of the Bahá'ís of Alaska with the author for many years.

Though sightless since early manhood, Eugene's keen insight, scope of vision, lustrous character and brilliance in radiating divine education and guidance are remarkable. He has given a preview of the fulfillment of 'Abdu'l-Bahá's prophecy: '*Should these Indians be educated and properly guided there can be no doubt that through the Divine teachings they will become so enlightened that the whole earth will be illumined*' (TDP 33).

His enlightenment has shed much illumination on consultation for this grateful servant, whose pleasure it is to dedicate this book to him.

Notes and Acknowledgements

This book attempts to discuss principles of consultation rather than to comment on administrative procedures. Anything not specifically mentioned in the Writings of the Central Figures of the Bahá'í Faith, or in the writings of the beloved Guardian or the Universal House of Justice, is regarded as a secondary issue. Unless the House of Justice indicates otherwise, each National Spiritual Assembly establishes procedures on secondary matters as best suits its circumstances; these are bound to differ from one area to another. If something mentioned in this book is different from the practice in any national community, it is because of this flexibility. It is not that one is right and the other wrong; it is a matter of choice. The procedures of any National Spiritual Assembly naturally take precedence in its own area of jurisdiction over any suggestions made here.

Quotations in the book are spelt in the way they appear in the source material, even though this gives rise to a number of inconsistencies with the rest of the text. Quotations from the Writings of the Báb, Bahá'u'lláh and 'Abdu'l-Bahá are printed in italics.

The role of women in the Bahá'í Cause is monumental. This, together with the fact that, according to the Bahá'í teachings, men and women are considered to be equal, makes it doubly regrettable that a pronoun referring to both sexes does not exist in the third person singular. Alas, there is none. In this book the editorial 'he' is used to indicate both sexes. There are three reasons for this: first, the constant use of 'he or she' is awkward and annoying; second, it follows the Guardian's usage; and third, it is the historically accepted use. Those who prefer to insert 'or she' wherever 'he' is used in the general sense should feel free to do so as that is what is meant.

* * *

There are many people whose assistance was vital in the writing of this book. First and foremost are the hundreds of people with whom I have consulted in various Spiritual Assemblies, committees and other settings over a span of 30 years. From these precious souls an appreciation of the sublime gift of consultation has been developed in the practical arena of everyday life.

The Hand of the Cause Dhikru'lláh Khadem and Mrs Khadem gave a great deal of encouragement to this project long before there was any serious thought of writing a book. I had been doing some work with Spiritual Assembly development since the early 70s. During consultation between Counsellor Velma Sherrill and the National Spiritual Assembly of the Bahá'ís of Alaska in 1979 a request was made that the work be committed to writing; without that request the long process which led to this book would never have started. Janet Smith, Blaine Reed, Tim Reed and Janet Stout played important roles during the preparation of a series of sixteen articles for the *Alaska Bahá'í News*. These were the forerunner of this greatly expanded volume and serve as its nucleus. Many helpful suggestions were made by Dr Jalíl Mahmoudi and Gleo Huyck who helped with the initial editing. Special thanks must go to Mike Fieldhouse for his ideas in design. Dr Khalil A. Khavari reviewed the first draft of the manuscript and made extensive recommendations which played a major role in the final text. The staff of George Ronald has been most helpful. Not the least among their contributions were suggestions for a more streamlined and sharpened presentation. Then there is my dear wife, Beverly. Her loving encouragement (she would not let me quit when I hit an unexpected obstacle), understanding, indulgence and direct assistance in many details have been a major sustaining factor.

To these, and to the many others too numerous to mention, go my deepest and profound thanks. Then, of course, there is you, dear reader. After all, this was done for you. If you find something of value within these pages, this labor of love will have fulfilled its purpose.

Introduction

Bahá'u'lláh, the Supreme Manifestation of God, while in exile, alone and with no apparent earthly power, reordered the whole basis of civilization. He proclaimed, '*Soon will the present day Order be rolled up, and a new one spread out in its stead*' (WOB 161). From that moment on things began to change. Slowly at first, then with increasing momentum, the process moves forward. Consider the following:

Absolute monarchy is nearly a thing of the past.

Religious leaders possess only a shadow of their former power and glory.

Long-established institutions of church and state, which once enjoyed the highest possible prestige, are losing the respect of the populace.

Cherished standards and traditions are increasingly challenged and are crumbling.

Chaos, confusion and upheaval are increasing daily.

The most enlightened and sincere statesmen seem powerless to resolve the problems of today.

Laxity in moral standards is weakening the very fiber of society.

All this was prophesied by the Blessed Perfection over a hundred years ago: '*From two ranks amongst men power hath been seized: kings and ecclesiastics*' (PDC 19). Now, as the old ways crumble, a new form of leadership is needed to fulfill those duties once performed by church and state.

In His Book of Laws, the Most Holy Book, the *Kitáb-i-Aqdas*, the Ancient Beauty established the institutions for regulating man's social life.

The Lord hath ordained that in every city a House of Justice be established wherein shall gather counsellors to the number of Bahá, and should it exceed this number it does not matter. It behooveth them to be the trusted ones of the Merciful among men and to regard themselves as the guardians appointed of God for all that dwell on earth. It is incumbent upon them to take counsel together and to have regard for the interests of the servants of God, for His sake, even as they regard their own interests, and to choose that which is meet and seemly. Thus hath the Lord your God commanded you. Beware lest ye put away that which is clearly revealed in His Tablet. Fear God, O ye that perceive. (BA 21, SCK 13)

A new structure is required. Administrative institutions are to be entrusted with providing order and stability for the world. The admonitions '*to take counsel together*', '*to have regard for the interests of the servants . . . and to choose that which is meet and seemly*' afford a protection that can liberate mankind from the scourge of corruption which has so plagued institutions of public trust in the past.

The delicate process of taking these lofty principles and putting them into practice makes a fascinating story. The blessed Báb gave the promise of the new day. Bahá'u'lláh established the laws and released the creative Spirit. 'Abdu'l-Bahá, the Center of the Covenant, clarified and explained in detail the agencies necessary to implement the new system, in His countless letters, public addresses, personal talks with pilgrims and in His Will and Testament. When the Master ascended and Shoghi Effendi became Guardian of the Cause of God, the necessary institutions were still largely non-existent or functioning in an elementary manner. It fell to this young man, still in his early twenties, to apply the divine principles and supervise the erection of the noble edifice so eloquently described by 'Abdu'l-Bahá.

He saw clearly that the administrative institutions which must support the Universal House of Justice needed to be developed first, before that Supreme Body could come into being. In a letter dated February 23, 1924, he explained that a period of transition was needed for Local and National Assemblies to develop and become strong. 'Not until these function vigorously and harmoniously can the hope for the termination of this period of transition be realized' (BA 63).

The new Guardian took several decisive and dramatic steps of far-reaching significance. The first was to give clear and concise instructions on the use of consultation, and the development of Local Spiritual Assemblies, in a letter dated March 5, 1922, and addressed: 'Dear fellow-workers in the Cause of Bahá'u'lláh'. Portions of this letter are examined more closely in Chapters 2 and 3.

Shoghi Effendi immediately began to develop the local and

national institutions of the Faith, but that story is outside the scope of this book. Suffice it to say that when the Universal House of Justice was elected for the first time in 1963, fifty-six National Spiritual Assemblies had been established as a result of the beloved Guardian's unremitting toil; now, in 1984, the Bahá'í world counts no fewer than 143 National Spiritual Assemblies – pillars of the Universal House of Justice – supported by approximately 30,000 Local Spiritual Assemblies. Bahá'ís reside in well over 100,000 centers in nearly 350 countries and dependencies of the world.

In the more than sixty years since the Guardian's letter of 1922, Bahá'ís the world over have been developing the institutions of the Faith while learning about consultation at the same time. Some lessons were learned easily and well. Others, it seems, must be learned over and over. In the development of the institutions there is stumbling, and sometimes clumsy use of consultation. Yet the Cause of God grows, the divine institutions develop, the consultative process matures with increasing strength and effectiveness. Generation after generation of new believers, some insecure and hesitant, many confident and eager, take their turn in this continuing drama.

The events of the past century-and-a-third clearly give ample evidence of two comforting facts. One is that protection from on high is guiding the destiny of this glorious Cause. 'Abdu'l-Bahá stated this sublime principle:

There is a power in this Cause – a mysterious power – far, far, far away from the ken of men and angels; that invisible power is the cause of all these outward activities. It moves the hearts. It rends the mountains. It administers the complicated affairs of the Cause. It inspires the friends. It dashes into a thousand pieces all the forces of opposition. It creates new spiritual worlds. This is the mystery of the Kingdom of Abhá! (CB 70)

Another awesome promise coming to fulfillment is that given by the Báb in His address to the Letters of the Living, when He told them to be *'assured of ultimate victory'* (DB 94). Subsequent events have clearly shown the onward march of the Cause toward that victory.

The transfer of power from the kings and ecclesiastics to the divine institutions continues unabated. Through consultation this process is propelling mankind ever closer to the Christ-promised fulfillment of *'Thy kingdom come. Thy will be done in earth, as it is in heaven'* (Matt. 6:10).

ONE

Take Ye Counsel Together

Consultation is one of the greatest bounties given to man. It is an art, a key which can unlock the mysteries of life and open the door to answers to the most perplexing questions – questions of intimate and personal concern, or questions of world-wide significance. It is a major tool for the coming-of-age of the human race, a fundamental element in the bringing into being of a new world civilization.

The development of the World Order of Bahá'u'lláh is frequently compared to the construction of a building. Bahá'u'lláh is the Divine Architect: He prepared the perfect plan. The Center of the Covenant, 'Abdu'l-Bahá, gave detailed instructions. The beloved Guardian, Shoghi Effendi, initiated and supervised the first stages. Now progress continues under the guidance of the Universal House of Justice.

The Bahá'ís of the world are the construction workers. By and large they lack the skills, experience and talent for such a momentous undertaking. They have the Teachings. They have the love and the spirit of this New Age. They have the Covenant. But how do they build a new world order? Where do they start?

They begin by preparing the material for the building project. Part of that material is consultation. In the words of 'Abdu'l-Bahá, '*The principle of consultation is one of the most fundamental elements of the divine edifice*' (CC no. 15).

To a degree Bahá'ís are familiar with consultation. Frequently, however, what passes as consultation is simply a reflection of the backgrounds of the people using it. Bahá'ís get into the habit of consulting in a certain way and assume that this is Bahá'í consultation.

As the Cause develops so must the understanding of this noble and precious tool.

The Lamp of Guidance

'Take ye counsel together in all matters, inasmuch as consultation is the lamp of guidance which leadeth the way, and is the bestower of understanding' (CC no. 1). With these choice words Bahá'u'lláh, the Supreme Manifestation of God for this Day, gave mankind this wonderful and powerful instrument for the handling of human affairs. Whether the matter be large or small, personal or public, simple or complex, consultation has the capacity to deal effectively with whatever the needs may be. It is a tool specifically suited to this modern age.

In considering the station of this magnificent gift from the Ancient Beauty, it is fascinating to ponder the descriptions of it found in the Writings. It is one of the *'two luminaries'* of the *'heaven of divine wisdom'*, the *'lamp of guidance'*, the *'bestower of understanding'*, the only means of attaining *'welfare'* and *'well-being'*, the bestower of *'greater awareness'*, the transmuter of *'conjecture into certitude'*, the *'shining light which, in a dark world, leadeth the way and guideth'*, that which makes manifest *'the maturity of the gift of understanding'*, *'a cause of awareness and of awakening'*, a *'source of good and well-being'* (CC 3).

'Abdu'l-Bahá clarifies some of the features of consultation: *'one of the most fundamental elements of the divine edifice'*, *'its result is light'*, the means of attracting *'the Grace of the Holy Spirit'*, of *'attracting the hosts of Divine confirmation'*. There will be an *'effect upon all the world'*, which will *'lead a world to eternal happiness'*, the *'hosts of the Supreme Concourse will render them victorious'*; it is the means of transforming a *'clash of thought'* into *'brilliant light'* which is the *'lightener of facts'*, *'one of the most potent instruments conducive to the tranquility and felicity of the people'*, the giver of *'insight'* enabling man to *'delve into questions which are unknown'*; it enables the *'light of truth to shine from the faces'*, it leads *'to the depths of each problem'* and makes it possible to find *'the right solution'* (CC 5–11).

A discussion about any part of the Creative Word is always exciting. The phrases *'bestower of understanding'*, *'greater awareness'* and *'luminary'* take on new dimensions, with richer and fuller meanings.

Consultation is a guaranteed and reliable means of obtaining the guidance, understanding, illumination and well-being mentioned above. What else comes with such high credentials?

There is both a revolutionary and an evolutionary element to consultation. It is revolutionary in that it is a dramatic change from anything known in the past, and is destined to change the affairs of mankind drastically. It is evolutionary in that it is the latest stage in the handling of human affairs.

There has always been a need for some system of conducting things, maintaining order, directing activities and settling differences. The most primitive system is the clash of strength: brute force against brute force.

The next stage is the clash of wills and vested interests. This improvement over knives and poisons, pits one set of determination against another. The term 'community of interests' is often used to describe areas of limited but common concerns. The clash of wills is especially effective within the limitations of a given community of interest. Vested interests clash with other vested interests in the hope that the best will win. In the political arena it demands freedom of speech and debate. The positions, pro and con, are argued so that choices can be made. In commerce this principle requires the free market place in which goods and services compete. For the scholar academic freedom is necessary so that positions may be presented, argued and supported by appropriate research. In civil disputes courts allow one side to confront another directly with assistance from advocates who present each side in the most favorable way. This same principle applies to other communities of interest.

The problem is that while issues can be settled by the clash of wills or vested interests in each respective area, decisions often have an impact far beyond those immediately involved. In this increasingly complex and interrelated world, few questions are merely political or only economic or strictly academic or purely legal. Only the system of consultation given by Bahá'u'lláh can reliably serve beyond those limitations. Unhampered by the restrictions of vested interests and the clash of wills, consultation among both interested and disinterested parties can place all issues in a more comprehensive perspective and assess implications much larger than those possible using only the areas of limited interest.

It is revolutionary in another sense. In recent history the best protection against the corruption of leadership has been pluralism and partisan politics. These served well during the rebellious, adolescent stage of development from which we are slowly emerging. But humanity is now on the threshold of maturity, in which unity supplants pluralism and partisan politics is replaced by consultation. In a pluralistic system each party or group claims it can solve the difficult problems of the day better than its opponents. Under consultation the best ideas can be used without worrying about who gets the credit. Rather than a clash of force, or a clash of wills, the system of Bahá'u'lláh permits the clash of ideas. Free from vested interests and corruption, this is the most advanced way. It is a system in which the genius of man will find full expression.

Consultation is also evolutionary in the sense that only gradually are its full potential, flexibility, use and powers being discovered and developed. As in the construction of a building, different parts of the divine edifice are reared in different ways. Sometimes discussion is ponderous and deals with difficult questions, like a large, important support beam or pillar being laboriously put into place. At other times consultation is punctuated by laughter and merriment. Those are the joyous decorations that add luster and beauty. Occasionally discussion degenerates into contention, argument and estrangement. Sometimes part of a building, too, has to be torn down and rebuilt until it's done right. But the building goes on, and all the activity, in the aggregate, demonstrates that *consultation is one of the most fundamental elements of the divine edifice*.

The process of consultation thus becomes the *'lamp of guidance'* which replaces the guidance once supplied by the institutions of church and state. It steps beyond the arenas of limited interest; it replaces brute force and contending vested interests; it allows man to graduate from the divisiveness of partisan politics. As these traditional devices become less and less effective their replacement is slowly maturing.

The Nature of Bahá'í Consultation

Consultation is both a means of jointly considering something and a means of allowing an idea to grow. There is a unique blend of experiences, knowledge, minds, hearts, feelings, hopes and fears. In a condition of suspended judgment these combine to allow the development of an idea, a transformation which comes about when there is a sincere exchange. Generally the final result is quite different from either the original thought or any of the specific additional contributions. It is neither a compromise nor the simple addition of one thought to another: it is a new creation.

Bahá'í consultation is a process characterized by these four features:

1. It releases creative energies from the minds and hearts of those involved.

2. New understanding and enlightenment are brought to a subject for a specific purpose such as to:

    solve a problem
    plan a course of action
    probe for deeper meanings
    generate inspiration
    gain new insights or knowledge
    examine other points of view
    reassess priorities and clarify purposes
    strengthen convictions

3. This is accomplished by a sharing and an interaction of appropriate information, ideas, thoughts, feelings and impressions – provided by the differing perspectives, knowledge, experiences, hopes and fears of those participating, and by allowing the interaction time to develop.

4. If this is done in an atmosphere fostering love, harmony and unity, it is Bahá'í consultation.

To summarize, Bahá'í consultation can be defined as a process for producing a change in order to accomplish some definite purpose. This involves a sharing and interaction of thoughts and feelings in a spirit of love and harmony.

This transformation can be compared to various changes in nature. In the mineral kingdom a variety of substances can combine to produce something different from and far greater than the mere sum of the parts. For example, under certain circumstances both sodium and chlorine can be poisonous. When chemically united they become something quite different from either – table salt – which is necessary to sustain human life.

Consultation can be compared to a growth process. An idea is like a seed. Proper temperature and moisture (spiritual conditions) are necessary for growth. A variety of elements are required in the soil for the seed to germinate and grow. The ultimate fruit may not have any of the characteristics of the seed or of the elements in the soil. Yet proper growth and maturity are not possible without these necessary, though dissimilar, items. These are like the different contributions made by those consulting. All play an important part, resulting in a new creation.

In order for the process of consultation to develop as intended, a great deal of patience, sacrifice, discipline, practice, desire to improve and, above all, love for and reliance on the Covenant are necessary.

The Universal House of Justice has pointed out, 'Consultation is no easy skill to learn, requiring as it does the subjugation of all egotism and unruly passions, the cultivation of frankness and freedom of thought as well as courtesy, openness of mind, and wholehearted acquiescence in a majority decision' (WG 96).

Happily, there is a wonder to this process. Even as the skill sharpens it proves its usefulness. Nor is its use limited to institutions: consultation is a valuable tool for families, businesses and professions, and can be used in personal, leisure and social affairs. Every Bahá'í – young or old, educated or illiterate, worldly-wise or naïve, veteran or newly enrolled – has the capacity to contribute to the development of this fundamental building material, and benefits personally in the process.

Fortunately, the Universal House of Justice has provided a great deal of material about consultation and its uses. Compilations on the Local Spiritual Assembly, Feasts, meetings and other topics have been made available to the Bahá'ís of the world. During the Five Year Plan an additional compilation was prepared on consultation. This has been published in the United States under the title, *Consultation: A Compilation*. (In the United Kingdom this same material was published under the title *The Heaven of Divine Wisdom*.)

The principle has been given to mankind – completely, thoroughly and eloquently. Now the potential must be developed.

The Bedrock of the World Order

In comparing the Cause of God to a building, mention is often made of '*pillars*', '*bedrock*', '*domes*', and '*foundations*'. Before the foundation of any building can be started, careful attention must be paid to what it is going to sit on.' Christ spoke of what happens when a house is built on sand rather than on rock (Matt. 7:24–27). Great care has been taken by Bahá'u'lláh to make sure that the foundation of His Divine Edifice rests on the best bedrock.

Bedrock is defined in *Webster's New International Dictionary* as 'solid rock beneath the soil or superficial rock', 'a secure foundation', and a 'basic principle or fact'.

The beloved Guardian, in his masterly word imagery, used the term bedrock for building the Bahá'í Administration. He referred to several things as being part of the bedrock of this peerless Order. Looking at these various items is fascinating as well as instructive. They blend together and relate to one another in a wonderful way: '. . . the bedrock of the Bahá'í administrative order is the principle of unity in diversity. . .' (DND 48); 'The bedrock on which this administrative Order is founded is God's immutable Purpose for mankind in this day' (WOB 156); '. . . basic . . . principles . . . laws and ordinances . . . constitute the bed-rock of God's latest Revelation to mankind' (GPB 281); 'Assemblies and not individuals constitute the bedrock on which the Administration is built' (USBN no. 80, Jan. 1934, p. 6). The 'National Fund [is] the bedrock on which all other institutions must necessarily rest . . .' (LBC 9); '. . . local Bahá'í community life . . . is the bedrock of Bahá'í national growth and development' (CBL no. 4); 'Consultation, frank and unfettered, is the bedrock of this unique order' (CC no. 32).

Analyzing these seven elements of bedrock, we find that two relate to goals or objectives:

the principle of unity in diversity

God's immutable Purpose for mankind in this day

three have to do with the structure of Bahá'í society:

laws, principles and ordinances

Spiritual Assemblies

the Fund

one is social:

Bahá'í community life

the other is the process through which all the rest ripen to maturity:

consultation

Unity in diversity

Contemporary thought tells us we should resolve our differences so that we can have unity. The Blessed Perfection tells us we should have unity so that we can make our differences harmonious. Contemporary thought tells us that unity is a lofty goal, an ideal if unattainable objective. The Covenant asserts that unity is the starting place, the necessary bedrock. This is a reversal of contemporary thought and perhaps one of the most far-reaching single innovations of this age.

There is no major problem which cannot be solved or accepted if we have unity. Conversely, there is no problem of significance which *can* have a lasting or meaningful solution without unity. Consider any of the major issues of the day. The problems which today's leaders are attempting to solve are perplexing. It does not matter if the issue is global, national or local; the right solution is elusive because there are vested interests and antagonistic factions seeking their own objectives. If those same people had unity of purpose they would be able to work out solutions which would prove beneficial to all.

Consultation under the protection of the Covenant serves to make unity possible, illuminates the real problems and makes evident their solutions.

God's immutable purpose for mankind

At first glance, this topic seems too big, too self-evident and too noble for effective consultation. However, it is a subject which should be addressed frequently and directly by the believers. Are the activities and projects into which so much energy is placed really serving the intended purpose?

Through consultation effectiveness can be separated from busyness. The proper objectives can be redefined and resources wisely used. Constant re-evaluation keeps the builders of the new World Order from being distracted and losing their sense of purpose and direction.

Principles, laws and ordinances

Equally important is the establishment of the '*principles, laws and ordinances*' of the Faith. These, too, are part of the bedrock required for the divine edifice, and can be nurtured by earnest and loving consultation. This is two-pronged. One is how each believer reflects these wonderful healing teachings in his own life. The other has to do with applying these teachings collectively through consultation.

Frequently there is more consultation on some of the restrictive laws than on some of the prescriptive laws. As early as 1922 the beloved Guardian warned about too much emphasis on what he called the 'negative' laws. For instance, some believers working in the areas of mass teaching are overburdened with the problem of alcohol. Frequently a great deal of time and consultation is spent on what to do about Bahá'ís who drink. That is a frustrating and generally fruitless exercise. Avoidance of alcohol is but one of the laws. Perhaps it would be more constructive to consult at length on some of the more positive and expansive laws such as the use of the obligatory and other prayers, child education, family unity, and teaching. Consultation on these subjects can produce a marvelous effect. The use of alcohol just may prove to be less of a problem when there is more consultation on the positive laws.

The Fund

That the Fund is considered an institution and that only Bahá'ís are allowed to contribute to it are two features which provide reasons for thoughtful reflection. Consultation is the means to consider the nature of the Fund, its increase and best use. This is sometimes an area of difficult, yet potentially rewarding, deliberation.

Spiritual Assemblies

Consultation is indispensable in the daily operation of the divinely ordained Spiritual Assemblies. This will be discussed more fully in Chapter 5.

Bahá'í community life

Social activities are not just a pleasant afterthought to the serious business of building a new World Order. A healthy, lively, dynamic community life is an integral part of that purpose: the joy, stability and security produced is a fundamental part of the bedrock. The growth of the Cause requires that serving it be done with a sense of shared joy and community spirit. Consultation makes that possible. In both formal and informal settings consultation can make all activities experiences of sharing, creating a natural sense of family.

Consultation

Consultation is the means, the catalyst, the mixer, the cement and 'one of the most fundamental elements of the divine edifice' because it allows for the development and maturing of all the other elements, while they, in turn, contribute to the development of consultation.

*　　*　　*

It is indeed a marvelous bedrock that the Ancient Beauty has provided for His new world. Those of us now standing on the threshold of this new age have the bounty of taking these raw ingredients and, through consultation, making of them the most sturdy, solid, secure foundation for all mankind.

TWO

How to Consult

Just three months after the Ascension of 'Abdu'l-Bahá the beloved Guardian wrote a long and detailed letter to the Bahá'ís of the West. A unique document, dated March 5, 1922, it describes Bahá'í consultation, giving specific instructions and stressing the importance and authority of Spiritual Assemblies. This letter, found on pages 17–25 of *Bahá'í Administration* and on pages 3–9 of *Unfolding Destiny*, should be studied carefully by all who wish to serve the Cause of Bahá'u'lláh today.

'Abdu'l-Bahá is frequently quoted in the letter. Of special interest are quotations found on page 21 of *Bahá'í Administration* and a long quotation on pages 22–3. These familiar passages give detailed instructions about consultation. Among the main features are the following:

A list of seven '*prime requisites*' for everyone who consults.

The two '*conditions*' necessary before consultation can take place.

The five rules of '*procedure*' which are the standard for all consultation.

Three steps in decision-making.

A list of topics about which to consult.

Six spiritual laws concerning consultation. These are stated as basic truths. They state cause-and-effect relationships with the certainty of the laws of nature, describing consequences. Four of these are warnings. The other two are promises filled with assurances and hope.

This chapter and Chapter 3 are based on the instructions from those passages.

The Prime Requisites

The spirit of those consulting together is the main factor that makes Bahá'í consultation unique. It is this that differentiates Bahá'í consultation from that among lawyers, doctors, boards of directors of civic groups, labor groups, business corporations, social and service clubs and professional organizations.

'Abdu'l-Bahá said that certain characteristics should be developed by 'them that take counsel together'. Who are the ones who 'take counsel together'? Naturally that includes members of Spiritual Assemblies, but it also includes anyone who will ever attend a Nineteen Day Feast, or go to school, or be part of a family. In other words, everyone.

What are prime requisites? The dictionary describes a requisite as something which is essential or necessary. Anything 'prime' is the first or most important. That means they are not just lofty but unattainable ideals; they are essential and necessary qualities which everyone must cultivate in order for consultation to develop properly.

Here is the passage:

The prime requisites for them that take counsel together are purity of motive, radiance of spirit, detachment from all else save God, attraction to His Divine Fragrances, humility and lowliness amongst His loved ones, patience and long-suffering in difficulties and servitude to His exalted Threshold. Should they be graciously aided to acquire these attributes, victory from the unseen Kingdom of Bahá shall be vouchsafed to them. (BA 21)

These are fascinating words. They have a beauty and poetry to them. They are not just words, however. They outline specific instructions which require close attention. When these qualities of the soul are developed by the individuals consulting, consultation blossoms into its full divine potential. Neglect these qualities and the spiritual conference remains nothing more than a lofty illusion.

The more progress individuals make in acquiring these attributes the better they consult. Furthermore, as time goes on and the Bahá'í community expands these attributes will become more abundant.

This will happen as the quality of Bahá'í life improves: with each generation those who consult should reflect these qualities to a greater degree. In the meantime, it is the responsibility of each Bahá'í to improve as much as possible in those qualities of character now. We cannot wait for worthier souls to arise – each individual must become worthier *now*.

In order to improve in these characteristics let us examine them closely. First, let us try to understand them. In thinking about them it seems that each item has several components. One aspect is a negative side which needs to be put aside. But beyond that is a positive potential to be developed. Next comes the step of making these positive aspects a natural part of our thinking. The final step is to make these characteristics a natural part of everyday life.

A few thoughts are suggested about each of the requisites:

1. *Purity of motive.* Motive is defined in the dictionary as 'an inner drive, impulse, intention, etc. that causes a person to do something'. Purity is defined as 'freedom from corrupting elements; clearness; unmixed'. On the negative side are: ulterior motives, multiple and mixed emotions and ego involvement. These need to be eliminated. Positive components include singleness of purpose and striving to win the good pleasure of Bahá'u'lláh.

2. *Radiance of spirit.* Radiance is defined as 'showing pleasure, love and well-being; sending out rays of light; shining brightly'. On the negative side it means doing away with a gloomy or pessimistic attitude. Happiness should be radiated and shared generously. Radiance involves a sensitivity to others, showing a genuine interest in their concerns, and pleasure in their triumphs and accomplishments. It is an enthusiasm for life. In consultation it is not usually so important how much one knows, as how much one cares. Cultivating the ability to find, nurture, and share happiness is necessary for effective consultation.

3. *Detachment from all else save God.* Being detached means 'not involved emotionally; impartial'. It does not mean indifference. It does mean deliberately setting aside personal preference and attachments and cultivating the quality of objectivity.

4. *Attraction to His Divine Fragrances.* The Divine Fragrances are found in all activities where there is the love of God. Attraction to those Fragrances implies a lively curiosity and interest in everything that relates to the Divine. It further implies not being attracted to

those things that appeal to the lower nature of man. Those who take counsel together should be informed about, find excitement in and give enthusiastic support to all Bahá'í projects, not just those which involve them personally. It also implies an eagerness rather than a reluctance to be together and consult. 'Abdu'l-Bahá stressed this principle in a preface to a prayer for Spiritual Assembly meetings when He said, *'Come ye together in gladness unalloyed . . .'* (USBP 138). Fortunately, with effort, anyone can develop this attraction.

5. *Humility and lowliness amongst His loved ones.* In Bahá'í consultation no one tries to exalt himself over another. A proud or boastful attitude is a negative element which needs to be curtailed. It undermines the very basis of this precious gift. Considering one's self as low and the others as high is a protection against vainglory and permits all contributions to be accepted on their own merits. On the other hand, in today's world humility is sometimes confused with weakness or timidity. In reality, there is a clear distinction between them.

Humility is not something one can strive for or achieve. Rather it develops to the degree that one is absorbed in divine attributes such as service to the Cause and to one's fellow-man. This service is really love in work clothes. True humility lies in the development and use of talents, capacities and resources that are necessary in the service of the Cause of Bahá'u'lláh. Then it is possible to rely on God and do the best one can energetically for the Cause without being self-conscious about it. The two-edged sword of fear and insecurity on the one side and pride or false modesty on the other awaits anyone who loses sight of true humility. The highest kind of strength, confidence and reliance in one's relationship to God is required to maintain the balance. Humility really rests in tirelessly giving all one's talents and energies in the path of God.

6. *Patience and long-suffering in difficulties.* Difficulties are an inescapable part of life. The question is how to meet them. 'Abdu'l-Bahá recommends patience – which should not be confused with inaction or being passive. Instead, it involves grace under stress – composure while deciding what action, if any, is appropriate. It means not being deluded by quick and easy solutions. Patience involves calm endurance and perseverance while waiting for results. It implies retaining self-control and perspective; persistence and diligence; and, above all, not succumbing to complaining and anger no matter what

frustrations are encountered. Long-suffering is 'enduring injuries, insults or trouble'. While everything reasonable is done to remove the source of difficulties, there is a need to recognize that some problems have no good solutions: they simply must be endured. Some unsolved problems are essential for our growth.

7. *Servitude to His exalted Threshold.* One meaning of servitude is '*being subject to a master*'. We are all subject to a wide variety of demands (see Chapter 8). But we can select our master from either the lower elements of life or a higher calling. 'Abdu'l-Bahá lovingly calls upon us to submit to our true Master, the Creator. The irony is that freedom is found only through this complete servitude. The people of Bahá, then, become distinguished by their freedom from ambitions and desires, from animalistic impulses, passions and greed, from a quest for mythical pleasure or self-gratification.

*   *   *

Obviously, no one has perfected any one of these seven qualities. It is reassuring that '*should they be graciously aided to acquire these attributes victory from the unseen Kingdom of Bahá shall be vouchsafed to them*'. As long as an earnest working and striving to improve in all these areas takes place, great benefit will accrue both to the individual and to the quality of consultation.

It is possible to make these prime requisites a natural part of life. Habits can be changed to reflect these qualities better. Aid in acquiring these virtues may come from many sources: tests and difficulties, encouragement and support from loved ones, deepening and serving the Cause. This aid is always available, but can only be used if there is a yearning for and acceptance of it. It is a sense of direction and process of growth which comes from conscious effort, development of love, unity and a sincere desire to serve. To help make these seven prime requisites a natural part of your own thinking make a list and place it somewhere where you will see it every day. Concentrate on one phrase at a time. Think about it. Discuss it with others. Figure out ways in which each of the requisites could apply to specific situations. Continue this each day with just one phrase for a week or a month or however long it takes for it to become a natural part of you. Then go on to the next.

No matter what else one does to prepare for consultation, the effort is incomplete until there is a deliberate attempt to improve in these essential characteristics which 'Abdu'l-Bahá referred to as the prime requisites.

The Two Conditions

In one part of the letter of March 5, 1922, the beloved Guardian quotes this fascinating passage written by 'Abdu'l-Bahá which establishes the conditions for consultation and describes the process and the results which will follow. In one paragraph six spiritual laws are stated with absolute certainty! He beautifully describes some cause-and-effect relationships. In this section the first part of that paragraph, which describes the two conditions, will be discussed.

Enumerating the obligations incumbent upon the members of consulting councils, the Beloved ['Abdu'l-Bahá] reveals the following: *The first condition is absolute love and harmony amongst the members of the assembly. They must be wholly free from estrangement and must manifest in themselves the Unity of God, for they are the waves of one sea, the drops of one river, the stars of one heaven, the rays of one sun, the trees of one orchard, the flowers of one garden. Should harmony of thought and absolute unity be non-existent, that gathering shall be dispersed and that assembly be brought to naught. The second condition:– They must when coming together turn their faces to the Kingdom on High and ask aid from the Realm of Glory.* (BA 22)

This quotation is familiar to most Bahá'ís, but it does not always get the attention it deserves.

A condition is defined as 'anything called for as a requirement before the completing of something else'. It is therefore necessary to look at these two conditions carefully, because they are required before there can be effective consultation.

Taking some parts of that passage separately, so that they can be seen in relationship to each other, may give a better picture of those conditions.

THE FIRST CONDITION

Absolute love and harmony amongst members of the assembly
Wholly free from estrangement
Manifest in themselves the Unity of God

They are

waves of one sea	*drops of one river*
stars of one heaven	*rays of one sun*
trees of one orchard	*flowers of one garden*

That first condition is awesome. From time to time Bahá'ís try to explain away the requirements. Statements have been heard such as, 'You have to love each other but you don't have to like each other', or, 'Manifesting the unity of God means being united in serving Bahá'u'lláh, not whether or not people get along with each other. You can't like everyone.'

These statements are short-sighted. The best that can be produced when those attitudes are present is a superficial unity, more of a truce than a unity. Being free from estrangement is far more than just tolerating someone. Antipathy towards the others with whom one is consulting has no place in Bahá'í consultation, no matter how it is rationalized, or even if it seems deserved. The unity of God must be reflected in the relationship of the believers towards each other, in or out of the council chamber. Absolute love and harmony include caring for each other in a personal way.

'Abdu'l-Bahá underscores the importance of this in the statement of the first of the six spiritual laws from this passage:

Should
harmony of thought and absolute unity
be non-existent
GATHERING SHALL BE DISPERSED
ASSEMBLY BE BROUGHT TO NAUGHT

This is a promise. Does it mean that the assembly will automatically be disbanded? Not necessarily. There are several questions to consider. One has to do with the difference between having absolute love and harmony and not having it. Another has to do with what absolute harmony really is. A third has to do with building upon whatever degree of unity does exist.

When ideal conditions are present, consultation flows freely, there is an easy movement into the depths of any question; discussion steps up to a higher plane. The effect can be compared to the use of the hydrofoil in boating. By means of this device a boat is lifted above the normal drag and friction of the water and proceeds with much greater ease and efficiency than would otherwise be possible. So, too, with consultation. When conditions approach the ideal, discussion becomes qualitatively different and glides along on a high plane unencumbered by petty matters which would otherwise form a drag and impede progress. A refreshing and exhilarating joy is experienced. For many people this is marked by a desire to linger after a session is over and an eagerness for the next meeting.

On the other hand, when estrangement enters, tension is produced. This tension creates a barrier to consultation which is like an invisible wall and very difficult to penetrate. Discussion becomes superficial and bogged down, and flounders in a sea of frustration. Decisions become surface and simplistic. The 'spiritual conference' (cc 10) of which 'Abdu'l-Bahá spoke is nowhere to be found. Many details are overlooked and unpleasantness often enters. Many people find it fatiguing to try to consult when love and harmony are missing. It drains the spirit and exhausts the nerves. Some people feel an urge to flee the premises and a reluctance to attend the next meeting. This often leads to excuses for missing meetings.

Even with limited unity assemblies do function and decisions are reached. But when unity is lessened, activities become mechanical and decisions faulty, and the joy and spirit are drained. There is still some hope. If only two members of the assembly have the vision of the preeminent station of consultation and have an intense yearning to serve the Beloved, there is some degree of unity which can be built upon and increased. Even if everyone is deprived of the vision of the assembly's divine station, that station still exists in the spiritual world of potential. If there is no growth toward 'absolute unity', the assembly will be 'brought to naught'. Among other things, that means that efforts will no longer produce results. Energies will be dispersed and rendered ineffective. Chapter 13 discusses what to do if estrangement persists.

THE SECOND CONDITION

| *turn their faces* | *to the Kingdom on High* |
| *ask aid* | *from the Realm of Glory* |

When people enter the council chamber everyone is thinking about something. Some will be thinking about their work, others about their families, leisure time activities, plans for after the meeting, their personal hopes, dreams, aspirations or problems – whatever. 'Abdu'l-Bahá states as the second condition that all must turn their faces, or attention and thoughts, in a single direction – to the Kingdom on High.

There are several techniques which can be used to accomplish this. One is to allow time for small talk and visiting before the meeting begins, or to ensure there is ample opportunity for a study class and/ or prayers prior to the consultation. Time spent in study and discussion of the Creative Word has a marvelously lubricating effect on consultation. (By the Creative Word is meant specifically the words of Bahá'u'lláh.) Other materials, no matter how appropriate for the agenda, do not produce the same results. Even studying administrative directives is not the same.

Topical material can be used, such as excerpts from the Writings on teaching, consultation, education, etc. Quotations concerning the spiritual life and the power of prayer are also appropriate. The *Hidden Words* or *Words of Wisdom* are excellent for this purpose, as are any of the many compilations now available.

This can be compared to musicians tuning up their instruments before a performance. It encourages a blending into harmony rather than allowing out-of-tune noise. If the transition period is neglected, consultation will be less effective and the tuning process will be hampered. Whatever it takes to turn people's thinking away from the everyday world to the Kingdom on High should be vigorously pursued.

The other part of the second condition involves asking aid – that is, an admission that we are incapable of doing the necessary work without assistance. The place to seek help is from the '*Realm of Glory*'. Not only is that proper; it is a necessary condition prior to consultation. The means of accomplishing this is through earnest prayer for assistance. Bahá'í consultation can begin only after these conditions have been met.

Procedures

Immediately after explaining the two conditions, 'Abdu'l-Bahá gives the five rules of procedure that are to be followed. '*They must then proceed with the utmost devotion, courtesy, dignity, care and moderation to express their views*' (BA 22).

These are the five simple rules of procedure:

Devotion

The Master begins with a description of what our attitude should be toward God and Bahá'u'lláh. In other words, consultation should be an expression of devotional life.

Courtesy

Both our attitude and our behavior toward one another should be crowned with courtesy. The Blessed Perfection said it was '*the prince of virtues*', a '*binding command*' (TB 88). It should therefore be the adorning of consultation. Differences of opinion are necessary. Yet any tendency towards rudeness must be resisted so that the princely virtue of courtesy remains the reigning condition.

Dignity

Following the proper attitudes towards God and one another is dignity. This is a reflection of how a person feels about himself. As a child of God this should be an attitude of respect for himself and dignity of manner and bearing, not to be confused with stuffiness. Each person is a noble creature of God. Consultation must reflect that human dignity with which each human being is endowed.

Care

The Center of the Covenant wants all matters to be presented with care. The implications of this are far-reaching. Sloppiness or lack of preparation has no place in Bahá'í consultation. Great attention should be paid to the details of what is being presented. The degree of thoroughness and care given any matter should reflect at least as high a standard as one would apply to his own personal affairs.

Moderation

While the foregoing qualities represent our attitudes towards God, each other, ourselves and the question at hand, moderation has to do with how items are presented. However, moderation should not be confused with indecisiveness or a lack of conviction.

Ideas should be put forth strongly and convincingly, but without forcing them on anyone. They are, rather, special contributions, worthy of consideration. The following statement by the Blessed Beauty is often thought of in connection with teaching, yet it also summarizes the essence of presenting a thought with moderation in consultation:

If ye be aware of a certain truth, if ye possess a jewel, of which others are deprived, share it with them in a language of utmost kindliness and good-will . . . A kindly tongue is the lodestone of the hearts of men. It is the bread of the spirit, it clotheth the words with meaning, it is the fountain of the light of wisdom and understanding . . . (GL 289)

Under these five rules of procedure, each individual is told to express his own views. It is not permissible to remain silent if the point of view which you hold has not yet been presented. Nor is it desirable to ask someone else to speak on your behalf. Advocacy is not a part of consultation. If someone else has already expressed your idea, it is not necessary to repeat it. But each one has the very specific responsibility to make sure that his views are known and expressed.

It is easy to forget some of these rules of procedure. If everyone would act as if 'Abdu'l-Bahá were in the room they would be more likely to consult according to this standard. One Spiritual Assembly puts out a chair for 'Abdu'l-Bahá and places His portrait on it as a reminder of how each one should conduct himself.

THREE

Making Decisions

The preceding chapter set the stage for making decisions. After work has been done on those instructions, the decision-making process itself may be started.

Parliamentary procedures, such as *Roberts' Rules of Order*, do *not* apply in Bahá'í consultation. This is not a criticism of such systems; they simply were not designed for the gift of consultation as established by the Blessed Beauty and are therefore inappropriate. For example, motions are not a necessary part of Bahá'í consultation, although they may be used if the group wishes. If a motion is to be made, it is only appropriate *after* discussion of the issue. In other systems, a motion is usually required *before* there can be discussion.

Collective Decision

A simple three-step procedure for making decisions can be inferred from 'Abdu'l-Bahá's Writings. The three steps are:

1. Understanding the situation
2. Deciding what to do
3. Executing or carrying out that decision

These steps are suggested in the letter of March 5, 1922 from the beloved Guardian. The Master also gives five more spiritual laws which relate to consultation. He calls attention to certain practices which should be followed and to some which are to be avoided.

They must in every matter search out the truth and not insist upon their own opinion, for stubbornness and persistence in one's views lead ultimately to discord and wrangling and the truth will remain hidden. The honored members must with all freedom express their own thoughts, and it is in no wise permissible for one to belittle the thought of another, nay, he must with moderation set forth the truth, and should differences of opinion arise a majority of voices must prevail, and all must obey and submit to the majority. It is again not permitted that any of the honored members object to or censure, whether in or out of the meeting, any decision arrived at previously, though that decision be not right, for such criticism would prevent any decision from being enforced. In short, whatsoever thing is arranged in harmony and with love and purity of motive, its result is light, and should the least trace of estrangement prevail the result shall be darkness upon darkness . . . If this be so regarded, that assembly shall be of God, but otherwise it shall lead to coolness and alienation that proceed from the Evil One. (BA 22)

A great deal is crowded into that short passage – so much, in fact, that it is easy to miss the straightforward description of consultation which is given.

There are many ways to analyze and understand this passage. It is an instructive and interesting exercise to make a diagram of these words, a chart showing how some of the ideas develop.

There is one especially interesting way to look at the word truth. It is used three times. While the second usage of the word is a caution, the first and third times it is used could be thought of as describing two quite different steps in a process, rather than simply being a repetition.

'Abdu'l-Bahá says to *'search out the truth'*. One may think of this as searching for the facts of the situation or problem. The statement *'set forth the truth'*, on the other hand, can be thought of as setting forth the solution or course of action.

It may be helpful to look at these different elements more closely.

STEPS IN THE DECISION-MAKING PROCESS
UNDERSTANDING
search out the truth
with all freedom express their own thoughts
DECIDING
with moderation set forth the truth
should differences of opinion arise
majority of voices must prevail
EXECUTING
all must obey and submit to the majority

The simplicity of the procedure is disarming. In fact, it is so simple, yet so complete, that its impact can be missed unless the steps are looked at closely.

Understanding

The Master starts with the explicit instructions that *'They must in every matter search out the truth . . .'* This implies being well enough informed to understand the real situation. In problem-solving it means knowing not only what happened but when, where, how and why. When consultation is used for the purpose of making plans, it means understanding what is to be accomplished, why and how it is to be done as well as considering the implications.

One of the most common mistakes, not only in Bahá'í consultation but in any kind of group action, is that people try to reach a decision before they understand the problem. In contrast to this, Bahá'í consultation requires that decisions are suspended or deferred until there has been full and frank discussion. This should not be confused with indecisiveness or vacillation. Instead it is a dynamic period for the incubation and development of ideas. For some people this is one of the most difficult aspects of Bahá'í consultation. However, by suspending judgment attention can be focused on the underlying issues out of which decisions emerge.

It seems that 'Abdu'l-Bahá is asking that great care be given to understanding those basic, underlying issues rather than seeking quick solutions. There are many things to consider such as:

Gathering and agreeing upon the facts. This implies sifting through and evaluating the relevant facts, fragments of information, misinformation and conflicting stories while discarding irrelevant facts.

Discovering the background. This involves determining whether or not the stated problem is the real one or if there is a more basic issue which needs to be addressed.

Seeing different perspectives. The same 'facts' can look quite different when seen from different points of view. What are the various perceptions of the 'facts'? How did those involved feel about the situation? How did they 'see' it?

Reviewing the Writings. All information must be reviewed in relationship to the Writings. Has guidance been given in this matter? What are the spiritual implications? How can the spiritual principles be applied? (It is a common trap to rely on

an experienced and knowledgeable Bahá'í or to try to apply
something out of context. If there is any doubt about what
the Writings say, look it up.)

Synthesizing information. Everything must be weighed and
brought together for a complete and accurate understanding.
The source material for this truth of the situation is varied. Some may
come from the knowledge of the individual members of the
consulting body. Information may be received from someone or
some institution not involved with the consultation. It may be necessary to table the matter for further investigation.

In explaining how to *'search out the truth'* 'Abdu'l-Bahá insists
there be free, open and frank discussion. The admonition to *'not insist
upon their own opinions'* speaks eloquently to this point. Once the
truth of the situation is established it may differ from previous opinions. Then, those other ideas must be re-evaluated.

Deciding

After there is a clear understanding of the situation, attention can be
turned to the solution. Once again the five rules of procedure are
important, as various solutions are suggested, discarded or modified.
When consultation has reached the point of conclusion, it is time to
formulate the agreed solution to the problem.

There are two ever-present dangers at this point. One is of trying
to come to a decision too quickly before there has been adequate
discussion. The other is the danger of talking beyond the point of
decision. In the first case the decision may prove inadequate. In the
second, when discussion continues beyond the peak moment of resolution, there is a danger that the decision can become diluted. The
crispest and most succinct decision generally comes the moment
consultation merges into a sharp focus of consensus. It is both an art
and a special talent to recognize that point of resolution. Fortunately,
with experience it becomes easier to recognize.

When it seems that the group has reached an answer to the
question under discussion, the chairman, or someone else so designated, should simply and clearly state that tentative decision. If the
group wants to have a motion made, someone could make the motion
at that time. The important thing is to bring the consultation to its
conclusion. The purpose is to have a clear and concise statement of

the decision which is being made so that all are agreeing to the same thing.

This moment of decision-making is a special occasion and generally the purpose of the consultation. The beloved Guardian gave a beautiful description of it: 'And, when they are called upon to arrive at a certain decision, they should, after dispassionate, anxious and cordial consultation, turn to God in prayer, and with earnestness and conviction and courage record their vote . . . ' (BA 64).

It may be that the consultation throughout has been an act of devotion or a form of prayer. In this case the group may choose not to have a separate prayer before finalizing every individual action. On the other hand, there are many times when the nature of the subject or the consultation has been such that it is desirable to have a special prayer before the vote is taken. Either way, it is important that the decision should be taken in the spirit of turning to God in prayer.

Once the tentative decision has been stated, and if it is apparent that everyone agrees, that becomes the decision and may be recorded as an action. If there is any doubt about consensus, a vote should be taken.

If there is no consensus, even if only one person seems not to agree, there are two courses of action available. One is to reintroduce the matter for further discussion. It may be that the consultation was inadequate. Many times, when the question is reopened, a new idea or different perspective comes to light which results in a revised and superior result. The group should be seeking the best answer, not just a decision.

The other possible action is to take a vote, abide by the majority decision, and go on to the next matter. While unanimity is preferred, it is not a requirement. It is not appropriate to spend a great deal of time trying to convince every dissenting member to agree just so that there can be unanimity. If everyone understands the situation and there is still a difference of opinion, then vote, record the decision and go on. The Center of the Covenant allowed for this when He said: '*If after discussion, a decision be carried unanimously well and good; but if, the Lord forbid, differences of opinion should arise, a majority of voices must prevail*' (BA 21-2).

It is worth pointing out that in Bahá'í consultation, unlike practically any other kind of deliberation, the only votes which count are votes in favor of the question. There are no nay votes and no abstentions. A person either votes in favor of the issue or does not. If a majority vote in favor, the matter carries. If a majority does not vote in favor, it does not carry.

*   *   *

In practice there may not be a clear distinction between understanding the problem and deciding what to do. Frequently the one blends into the other. While understanding is developing, the decision, in some rudimentary form, is often taking shape. Moreover, the key to the solution often lies in the problem itself. When there is a proper understanding of the situation the solution often becomes self-evident.

In both understanding the problem and deciding what to do full and frank discussion is required. Ideas must be given with all freedom following the five rules of procedure. This is the heart of consultation – and this is where the sparks fly: '*The shining spark of truth cometh forth only after the clash of differing opinions*'(BA 21). Without opinions clashing there can be no spark of truth. The thing to be remembered is that it is the opinions, not the people or personalities, which must clash. Another point is to look at the spark, not the clash. Opinions must be stated strongly enough, but kindly, so that they *can* clash with another opinion.

A key to this process is to remain emotionally detached from any contribution made. Once it is expressed, the idea belongs to the group. It can then be beat upon, pummeled, re-examined and mauled until it is virtually unrecognizable. Then sparks of truth will shine! If one holds on to the comments he has made as his own and retains some pride of authorship, the clashes will cause hurt feelings. Then conflicting ideas no longer make sparks of truth, they lose their virtue. Look for the brilliant light. Avoid the clash which produces more heat than light. When that happens the group has been de-railed from the track of consultation and the truth remains hidden.

If productive discussion has been exhausted and no clear consensus is apparent, the group may wish either to make an arbitrary decision and move on or table the matter for later consideration.

Executing
Even though a decision can be reached by a majority vote, once a

conclusion is reached it is no longer simply a '*decision of the majority*'. It is of the whole group. Then come the extremely important requirements that (1) it is not permitted to criticize the decision either in or out of the meeting and (2) everyone is under the obligation to help carry it out and make it work. Making it work is part of the decision. Decision-making is not really consummated until the task is performed. This puts a heavy obligation on the consulting group to make sure that what is decided can actually be achieved. When the Master says '*all must obey and submit to the majority*', it is a spiritual obligation. It is therefore extremely important that the consulting group does not impose tasks which are impossible or unlikely to be carried out. Nor is it wise to ask an individual to do something which is truly contrary to his personal interests or something which is self-defeating or beyond his capability. Asking someone to do something which is contrary to previous instructions should also be avoided. While individuals carry things out, responsibility for success or failure really belongs to the consulting group.

'Abdu'l-Bahá said: '*The most memorable instance of spiritual consultation was the meeting of the disciples of Jesus Christ upon the mount after His ascension.*' Then He explained how they discussed the situation and the tasks which had to be performed. They agreed what was to be done. '*Then they descended from the summit of the mountain and each went forth in a different direction upon his divine mission*' (CC no. 22). Their actions validated the consultation.

Everyone has the obligation to do his very best to make the decisions work. It does not matter how the person voted.

Intermingled with these steps, several undesirable practices are mentioned which are to be avoided. The Center of the Covenant admonishes those consulting:

> *Not [to] insist upon their own opinion*
>
> *It is in no wise permissible for one to belittle the thoughts of another*
>
> *Not permitted that anyone of the honored members object to or censure any decision in or out of the meeting though that decision be not right*

He also states another spiritual law of consultation:

stubbornness and persistence
lead to
discord and wrangling
and the truth will remain hidden

Just as certain as any physical law, stubbornness and persistence will lead to discord and wrangling. Unfortunately that is not the end of it. As a result of this action 'Abdu'l-Bahá guarantees that *'the truth will remain hidden'*. That is no idle threat; it follows discord and wrangling with perfect reliability. It is impossible to discover the truth as long as discord and wrangling continue.

Four more spiritual laws are presented at the end of this passage. One is the statement that *'criticism would prevent any decision from being enforced'*. This has far-reaching implications for the future of mankind. In this day when cynicism and criticism of everything that has anything to do with public policy are so common it is a hard but rewarding discipline to operate in an atmosphere where criticism, by religious decree, is forbidden!

Another spiritual law from this passage is a refreshing and rewarding one: *'whatsoever thing is arranged in harmony and with love and purity of motive, its result is light.'* Nothing is said about how good the decision is, or the brilliance or ingenuity of the ideas presented, rather it is the spirit which is important. 'Abdu'l-Bahá adds an extra promise in the assurance that *'If this be so regarded, that assembly shall be of God . . .'*

In contrast to that: *'should the least trace of estrangement prevail the result shall be darkness upon darkness . . .'* With another absolute promise the Center of the Covenant warns that under those conditions there shall be *'coolness and alienation that proceed from the Evil One'*. A bad decision or even incompetence does not cause severe problems: estrangement does.

The final spiritual law is a most encouraging one:

Should they endeavor to fulfill these conditions the Grace of the Holy Spirit shall be vouchsafed unto them, and that assembly shall become the center of the Divine blessings, the hosts of Divine confirmation shall come to their aid, and they shall day by day receive a new effusion of Spirit. (BA 22–3)

It may be easier to grasp this if the comments are grouped a little differently.

> *Should they* ENDEAVOR *to fulfill these conditions*
> *Grace of the Holy Spirit shall be vouchsafed*
> *Assembly shall become the center of the Divine blessings*
> *Hosts of Divine confirmation shall come to their aid*
> *Day by day receive a new effusion of Spirit*

To win these blessings it is not necessary to reach the best possible decisions or to be perfect in deliberations. All that is necessary is to ENDEAVOR to fulfill the conditions. This means the blessings are equally available to the novice and the seasoned veteran so long as the proper spirit and the endeavor is there. This is another absolute promise.

Who Makes the Final Decision?

Not all consultation results in a group decision. There are three situations using consultation, differing according to who makes the final decision: (1) collective decisions; (2) decisions by appointed individuals; (3) no decisions, except personal.

Collective decisions

In many situations common to Bahá'ís the principle is applied that the views of the majority shall prevail. These include Spiritual Assemblies (and usually their committees); the institution of the Feast and the institution of the National Convention. The general method for collective decision has been outlined in the preceding section.

Appointed individuals

Consultation is often used even when a majority vote is clearly inappropriate. The most outstanding example of this principle was the institution of the Guardianship. The Guardian consulted with a great number of people on many matters. But decisions were always his and his alone.

In the institutions of the Hands of the Cause, the Counsellors, and the Auxiliary Board there is also a great deal of consultation. There are some collective conclusions but many of the decisions made by members of these institutions are individual ones. Further, these decisions are usually advisory in nature rather then executive.

In other situations, such as the institution of the Summer School, institutes, teaching and other projects, a leader or committee is appointed by some governing institution. In these cases guidance and instructions have been given by that institution. In order to carry out these instructions there must be on-the-spot authority, which must rest with the individual(s) in charge rather than with a majority of those participating. This in no way contradicts any principle of the Faith; it is a means of carrying out the instructions of the sponsoring institution. Here consultation takes place at two levels. One is the consultation required to develop the guidance and instructions given to those in authority. The other is the consultation of the designated leader(s) with the participants. In the second situation the final decisions rest with the appointed leader(s). If majority rule by the participants were permitted it could completely change the intentions of the sponsoring institution and create confusion. It could undermine the authority of the Spiritual Assembly, Teaching Committee or whoever the sponsoring body may be.

For example, a Spiritual Assembly may assign to someone the task of explaining the Nineteen Day Feast to a children's class. The class may prefer to talk about going on a picnic. The teacher may or may not consult with the class but the teacher, not the class, must be the one to decide what to discuss, or there is the danger that the class would unwittingly defeat the intent of the Spiritual Assembly. All this would be done through majority rule, and it would be wrong.

No group decision

A great many situations arise where consultation may be used but is not intended to lead to a decision. Among these are the third, or social, part of the Feast, conferences, workshops, deepening sessions and schools. In this context consultation is a means of illumination, of understanding and of developing certitude.

This type of consultation is in many ways like other discussions, but there is an important difference. When the intent is to enlighten, understand a truth, or gain a better perspective, and this is done with an attitude of sharing, of promoting love and harmony, it is consultation. Otherwise it is merely conversation.

The social part of a Feast or an informal moment at Summer School serve as good examples of how this works. One of the friends may start to talk with two or three others about something in the Writings. As they discuss the topic new insights are often found. A hazy understanding may become clear. Inspiration on how to handle a difficult matter may become apparent. This simple procedure has become the means for the maturing of an idea. It is also a literal fulfillment of the description of consultation from the Pen of Bahá'u'lláh. The underlying purpose of all Bahá'í consultation is to promote unity, love and harmony. 'Abdu'l-Bahá said: '. . . *true consultation is spiritual conference in the attitude and atmosphere of love. Members must love each other in the spirit of fellowship in order that good results may be forthcoming. Love and fellowship are the foundation'* (CC no. 22).

FOUR

Improving Consultation

Spiritual principles and commitment give Bahá'í consultation its distinctive quality. Yet there are some other practical items which facilitate the flow of discussion. These help build and maintain a framework within which the spiritual basis of consultation can function at its best.

Necessary Skills

The subject matter of this section is vast and there is no attempt here to treat it in detail.

Talking (used here to mean all aspects of expression, both verbal and non-verbal, including pauses, body language, inflections and facial expressions, connotations and denotations), listening (which includes all aspects of reception and observation), and communication (which should be the aim of the first two, including all aspects of sharing information, ideas, feelings and impressions or conveying a message) are the basic tools of all social behavior. These skills are also the basic tools of consultation. However, they are not by themselves consultation. For instance, communication is used in ordinary conversation, but that is not necessarily consultation. The difference depends on the purpose. Let us briefly consider these 'basic tools' and how they relate to consultation.

Talking

In addition to speaking clearly, distinctly and loudly enough so that everyone can hear without straining, there are some other points which should be mentioned about talking as a part of consultation:

1. *Speak to the point.* Hedging, hinting, being obscure or coy, using indirect or veiled language, simply invite misunderstandings and make consultation more difficult. The more clear, concise, logical, simple and directly related to the point the comments can be, the better. Even thinking out loud need not be rambling. Be specific.

2. *Feelings count.* Express feelings even if you do not have a clear understanding of why you feel the way you do. It is perfectly all right to simply say, 'I don't know why, but there is something about that I like (or don't like).' It's amazing what a valuable contribution such a simple and honest statement can make.

3. *Background.* Sometimes, but not always, the reason(s) for an opinion are as valuable as the opinion itself. Giving extra information may be tedious, unnecessary, time-consuming and counterproductive; on the other hand, there are times when it is vital to the consultative process. Give additional information when necessary for others to grasp what you are saying. They need not agree with you. It is not your purpose to convince others you are right, but they need to understand you. Examples are helpful.

4. *Include everyone.* Speak to the whole group. If someone does not have the background to understand what is being said, give the necessary information. Hidden meanings have no place. The idea is to inform everyone to the level of understanding necessary to make an intelligent decision. When one or more are ill-informed the results will be inferior.

5. *Courtesy.* Basic respect for the others should always be apparent even when there are strong differences of opinion. The courtesy with which we treat one another is a measure of the degree to which Bahá'u'lláh's teachings have touched our hearts because He has commanded it. Speak in consultation as if 'Abdu'l-Bahá were present.

Listening

Effective listening is one of the most underdeveloped skills of present-day man. Creative listening – that is listening for a specific and intended purpose – is practically unheard of. Yet the ability to listen attentively is a mark of maturity and fundamental to consultation.

It is not my intention here to analyze listening and all its fascinating aspects. What is of concern is how listening affects consultation.

Without effective and creative listening, there is no consultation. Here are a few points to think about:

1. Listen as if you cared. If you want people to know what you say, it is only fair to listen earnestly to what they say. In fact, each individual makes a greater contribution to consultation by the quality of his listening than is generally realized. Being indifferent, preoccupied, or fidgeting as others speak is a sure way of reducing the effectiveness of the consultation. One believer reported an experience of meeting with the Universal House of Justice. She said she had never felt 'so listened to' in all her life. The caring demonstrated in the quality of their listening affected her deeply and aided her in the quality of her reporting. Good listening is amazingly supportive. A good listener contributes to the flow of potentially valuable wisdom. An old adage holds that a good listener is the cause of blossoming in a speaker.

2. Listen for the feelings as well as the ideas which are presented. Listen as if you had to report to 'Abdu'l-Bahá exactly what the speaker was feeling and trying to convey.

3. Think about the purpose of the consultation. When you are consulting, everything that is being said should relate to that purpose.

4. Do not waste a lot of energy looking for hidden meanings or concealed motives, nor trying to analyze the nuances of expression. An attempt to scrutinize too carefully the feelings behind the words or the shift in mood may interfere with the freedom of the consultation. It invites the pursuing of secondary issues at the expense of the main purpose. Keep thoughts focused on the purpose of consultation, and never mind the interesting diversions.

Communicating

The essence of communication is sharing information, understanding, feelings and impressions. The greater the sense of unity and sense of common purpose, the easier effective communication becomes. Here are a few things which contribute:

1. *Acceptance.* A genuine feeling of love and acceptance must be evident. No one communicates very well in a group in which he does not feel accepted or in which he feels his contribution does not matter. There is no room for a feeling of exclusiveness or superiority/ inferiority in Bahá'í consultation.

2. *Eye contact.* Whether or not and how there is eye contact affects communication. The effect varies from person to person and from

culture to culture. For some, eye contact communicates concern. There are some cultures in which that is not true, and there are some individuals who feel uncomfortable with continual eye contact. The correct way is to do whatever puts people at ease and improves consultation in the group concerned. Continual eye contact is not necessarily a demonstration of sincerity.

3. The differences between communication and effective consultation must be kept in mind. Many details may contribute to communication, including whether people are sitting around a table or seated more casually on comfortable chairs. Do whatever is appropriate to improve communication as it affects the consultation.

* * *

Consultation requires the disciplined use of communication skills. The germ of an idea needs to develop through changes resulting from each contribution. The ideal is to produce the best possible results that can be obtained from the minds, the backgrounds, the feelings and hearts of those participating. Consultation has a purpose; talking, listening and communication are the skills which can move an idea toward that objective. Yet no matter how well-developed these skills are, they do not result in consultation if they do not contribute toward the goal.

The rewards of developing the art of consultation are great:

If a few souls gather together in a beloved meeting with the feelings of the Kingdom, with the divine attractions, with pure hearts and with absolute purity and holiness, to consort in spirit and fragrance, that gathering will have its effect upon all the world. The conditions, the words and the deeds of that gathering will lead a world to eternal happiness and will be an evidence of the favors of the Kingdom. The Holy Spirit will strengthen them and the hosts of the Supreme Concourse will render them victorious and the angels of Abhá will come in succession. (CC no. 11)

Points to Remember

Institutions, like individuals, develop habits. By changing some habits of procedure renewed vigor can sometimes be given to the institution. Here are some simple techniques which can make a major difference in bringing freshness to consultation.

Consult on the problem itself. By energetic discussion many additional ideas can be generated, bringing new life into the consultation.

It may be that some small changes can be made which will make some major differences.

Some people may do the same job extremely well year after year. However, there may be an advantage in making some personnel changes on different committees just to introduce new perspectives. Care must be exercised so as not to interfere with an effective program just for the sake of change.

Fresh ideas, activities and approaches can be generated through 'brainstorming' sessions. An assembly may wish to do this itself or invite others to participate. An excellent idea is to invite the community as a whole or select members to exchange thoughts on a specific subject. This does two things: first, it gives fresh perspective to the assembly; secondly, by sharing its concerns the assembly generates support and enthusiasm from community members to a truly exciting degree.

Assemblies, like people, get into a rut and develop habits which suppress creativity. By experimenting with some of the simple techniques mentioned above a new vitality may result. The idea is to use the mechanics of consultation to enhance creativity, not to impede it.

*   *   *

The following lists of suggestions are, in part, a summary of the things discussed so far. They include some specific and simple things which can have a beneficial effect on consultation.

Before the event:
  1. Know the reason you are meeting and the importance of what you are doing.
  2. Pray for the success of the meeting.
  3. Ask others, who may not be attending, to pray for the success of the meeting.
  4. When approaching the meeting itself, pray and meditate on one of the prime requisites, or something else from the Creative Word.

During the meeting:
  5. Make sure physical arrangements are appropriate (e.g. reasonably comfortable, minimum of distractions, enough light, writing material, etc.).

6. Allow for a transition from the differing thoughts of the nether world to the united thoughts of the Divine.

7. Remember that all are doing Bahá'u'lláh's work. Speak as if He were listening.

8. Say the Greatest Name silently while waiting for others to speak.

9. Listen carefully. Listen not just to the words but to what the speaker is trying to convey. Listen to hear the spirit of what is meant. If the meaning is unclear, ask for clarification.

10. Each must think at least as seriously about what others say as about what he says himself.

11. In both speaking and listening strive not to offend, and guard against being offended.

12. In speaking respect the time of others. Present the idea or information clearly without rambling or bringing up unnecessary information, no matter how interesting. Do not merely repeat what others have said.

What if the spirit fades?

13. Try to discover and resolve the reason why the spirit is fading.

14. If something is bothering one or more persons present, bring it up and discuss it. Don't let it fester and pull the general spirit down.

15. Remember and remind one another that all are Bahá'ís and all really desire the same result.

16. Remind yourself and others of the seven requisites, two conditions and five rules of procedure outlined by 'Abdu'l-Bahá.

17. As a group redefine and refocus on the purpose for that particular meeting, and the larger purpose which is being served.

18. Ask for one or more prayers.

19. A period of silence may be appropriate.

20. Try to resolve conflicts so that no one leaves with strained feelings.

21. If there is a continuing problem, everyone should pray, even more ardently, between meetings that the problem may be resolved. (This extremely important issue is discussed more fully in Chapter 13.)

After the meeting:

22. Be thankful for having been given an opportunity to be of service.

23. Remind yourself of the importance of what you are doing.

24. If you have been given a task to perform, plan immediately when and how you will do it.

25. Pray for the success of all decisions which were made.

26. Be ready to assist others who have specific tasks to perform if the occasion arises.

27. Be alert to all situations or information which will be of use for the next meeting and prepare yourself spiritually for that meeting.

Summary

This summary of Chapters 2, 3 and 4 is based on quotations from 'Abdu'l-Bahá found in *Bahá'í Administration*, pp. 21–3, where He sets out those necessary elements which make Bahá'í consultation different from other types of group decision. Discussion of these quotations is recommended.

1. Each individual who would be part of consultation should: (a) study; (b) meditate on the inner meaning; (c) discuss with others; and (d) strive to acquire a fuller measure of those seven virtues described by 'Abdu'l-Bahá as '*the prime requisites for them that take counsel together*':

    i.   Purity of motive

    ii.   Radiance of spirit

    iii.   Detachment from all else save God

    iv.   Attraction to His Divine Fragrances

    v.   Humility and lowliness amongst His loved ones

    vi.   Patience and long-suffering in difficulties

    vii.   Servitude to His exalted Threshold

2. When coming together two essential conditions must be established:

    i.   *Absolute love and harmony amongst the members . . .* 'This implies resolving or at least looking beyond any differences which exist; forgiving and forgetting; and developing a condition of anxious and genuine concern for one another.

    ii.   '*Turn their faces to the Kingdom on High and ask aid from the Realm of Glory.*' Starting with one or more prayers and meditating on or discussing other items from the Writings are ways to bring about this process.

3. All discussions must follow the five rules of procedure:

    i.   *devotion*

    ii.   *courtesy*

    iii.   *dignity*

iv.   *care*

v.   *moderation*

4. Different points of view must be freely expressed and judgments suspended in order to:

i.   *'Search out the truth'* by arriving at an adequate understanding of the situation, problem or project under discussion. This includes establishing and evaluating the facts as well as candidly discussing their implications.

ii.   *'Set forth the truth'* through developing trial solutions and finally arriving at the best decision or course of action in the light of all the relevant circumstances.

5. *'All must obey and submit to the majority'* by giving whole-hearted acceptance and support to the decision once it is made, by doing whatever is necessary to make the decision work.

The degree to which those consulting *'endeavor to fulfill those conditions'* will determine the extent to which *'that assembly shall be of God'*. Conversely, the degree to which one or more of the above items is neglected will determine the extent to which *'that gathering shall be dispersed and that assembly brought to naught'*. The consequences, for better or for worse, are foreordained.

FIVE

Spiritual Assemblies

The principles establishing the institution of the Spiritual Assembly come from the Supreme Manifestation of God Himself. This towering institution has no counterpart in any existing system of governance. It has simple lines of communication and sound structure; however, it cannot function properly unless there is a spiritual atmosphere and commitment. In the words of the Guardian, it serves 'only as an instrument to facilitate the spirit of the Faith out into the world' (PBA 14).

Spirit

The unique character of the Spiritual Assembly calls for special attention to the spiritual basis of that majestic edifice. This is nowhere better described than in the prayer which the Master revealed for the 'House of Spirituality' (Spiritual Assembly) of Chicago. The beloved Guardian translated this prayer and included it in his long letter of March 5, 1922: the prayer was thus included in one of his first administrative directives to the Western World.

A study of the prayer is highly revealing. It is more than words for ceremonial use at the beginning of a meeting. It sets the tone, the style, the purpose and the desired results of the Spiritual Assembly. It provides insight into the sacred tasks.

The first nine words are especially interesting: '*O God, my God! We are servants of Thine . . .*' (BA 20). These first two words (*O God . . .*) are an invocation and a statement of Divine Nature. The second two (*my God!*) shows the personal relationship each member has with his Creator. There is nothing vague about it. It is clear, definite and personal. This is followed by an exclamation mark showing both strong feeling and a sense of completion.

With the fifth word (*We*) a new relationship enters. There is a change from the first person singular to the first person plural. Everyone steps over the threshold of his individual relationship with God; the participants enter a united condition. With it comes a corporate, or single and united mind – a new entity, different from and superior to the sum of the nine parts.

The sixth and seventh words (*are servants*) proclaim the station of servitude which is the highest station for man. '. . . *of Thine*' clearly implies servitude to God.

Further on in that prayer the reason why the members have been brought together is stated: purposes have been harmonized '*to exalt Thy Word amidst mankind*'. Every time that Assembly meets and that prayer is used there is the reminder that the fundamental reason all are together is to exalt the word of God. This can be accomplished when each one is in harmony with the other, with the aim of producing a corporate and balanced whole.

Towards the end of the prayer is the request that thoughts, views and feelings may become as one '. . . *manifesting the spirit of union throughout the world*' (BA 21).

Functioning in the manner indicated in that prayer is best accomplished by taking seriously the advice of the beloved Guardian:

Let us also bear in mind that the keynote of the Cause of God is not dictatorial authority but humble fellowship, not arbitrary power, but the spirit of frank and loving consultation. Nothing short of the spirit of a true Bahá'í can hope to reconcile the principles of mercy and justice, of freedom and submission, of the sanctity of the right of the individual and of self-surrender, of vigilance, discretion and prudence on the one hand, and fellowship, candour, and courage on the other.

The duties of those whom the friends have freely and conscientiously elected as their representatives are no less vital and binding than the obligations of those who have chosen them. Their function is not to dictate, but to consult, and consult not only among themselves, but as much as possible with the friends whom they represent. They must regard themselves in no other light but that of chosen instruments for a more efficient and dignified presentation of the Cause of God. They should never be led to suppose that they are the central ornaments of the body of the Cause, intrinsically superior to others in capacity or merit, and sole promoters of its teachings and principles. They should approach their task with extreme humility, and endeavour, by their open-mindedness, their high sense of justice and duty, their candour, their modesty, their entire devotion to the welfare and interests of the friends, the Cause, and humanity, to win, not only the confidence and the genuine support and respect of those whom they serve, but also their esteem and real affection. They must, at all times, avoid the spirit of exclusiveness, the atmosphere of secrecy, free themselves from a domineering attitude, and banish all forms of prejudice and passion from their deliberations. They should, within the limits of wise discretion, take the friends into their confidence, acquaint them with their plans, share with them their problems and anxieties, and seek their advice and counsel. And, when they are called upon to arrive at a certain decision, they should, after dispassionate, anxious and cordial consultation, turn to God in prayer, and with earnestness and conviction and courage record their vote and abide by the voice of the majority, which we are told by our Master to be the voice of truth, never to be challenged, and always to be wholeheartedly enforced. To this voice the friends must heartily respond, and regard it as the only means that can insure the protection and advancement of the Cause. (BA 63-4)

Form

The form of the Spiritual Assembly is deceptively simple. There are nine members elected annually (at this present stage in the development of the Faith). Once elected each member has the same authority and rights as every other member. No one enjoys special privileges due to the number of votes received, office held or length of service. Individual authority or power do not exist. There is thus no temptation to try to gain control.

Who should serve on Spiritual Assemblies? The qualifications for membership are indeed lofty and no one totally fulfills them. The qualities to look for were clearly described by the Guardian: '. . . those who can best combine the necessary qualities of unquestioned loyalty, of selfless devotion, of a well-trained mind, of recognized ability and mature experience' (BA 88).

Even so, in many communities today the real question is 'Who is available?' As the Faith grows and there are larger numbers to choose from who better reflect the desired qualities, Spiritual Assemblies will improve accordingly. In the meantime, the Universal House of

Justice and Spiritual Assemblies remain the only chosen instruments of promised guidance to which all must turn.

The challenge at this stage is to develop the institution within the framework provided using the available resources and dealing with the problems of the day. There is a need to be efficient and use sound administrative procedures, but that cannot be an end in itself. The following was written on behalf of the Guardian:

Administrative efficiency and order should always be accompanied by an equal degree of love, of devotion and of spiritual development. Both of them are essential and to attempt to dissociate one from the other is to deaden the body of the Cause. In these days, when the Faith is still in its infancy, great care must be taken lest mere administrative routine stifles the spirit which must feed the body of the Administration itself. That spirit is its propelling force and the motivating power of its very life.

But as already emphasized, both the spirit and the form are essential for the safe and speedy development of the Administration. To maintain full balance between them is the main and unique responsibility of the administrators of the Cause. (NSA 57–8)

Leadership

While in the prison city of 'Akká the Ancient Beauty provided the world with a new form of leadership in His Most Holy Book, the *Kitáb-i-Aqdas*. Bahá'u'lláh called these leaders *'the trusted ones of the Merciful'* and said they were *'to have regard for the interests of the servants of God (and) . . . choose that which is meet and seemly'* (SCK 13).

This extraordinary form of leadership freed the rank and file of mankind from silence. Now their voices could be heard in the affairs which affected them. It freed them from the domination of the arrogant who abused authority. It freed the human spirit from isolation by creating new channels of expression.

To make this liberation possible some dramatic changes were required. The system established by the King of Glory removed the mantle of leadership from those who would seek it and thrust it upon others, many of whom would really rather not be involved. In a different setting these souls would be able to avoid the burdens and responsibilities which come with leadership.

There are many distinctions between Bahá'í administration and other more traditional types. First of all, in Bahá'í settings, there is the obligation to create and maintain the proper spiritual conditions. Also, in most systems of administration people seek the offices to be held. Often this is for some self-serving purpose such as glory, financial reward, prestige, power, special privileges, etc. In contrast, the Bahá'í system makes it extremely difficult for a person to seek a position. Rather, it is the position which seeks out the individual.

An interesting situation is created for believers who are selected to serve in the institutions of either the 'rulers' or the 'learned' (see p. 68). Some, even though they did not seek the role, find this form of service a source of great pleasure and satisfaction. It is as if they have a natural aptitude and disposition for these activities. For them it is a wonderful and rewarding experience. They are fortunate and serve well as long as they maintain proper perspective. Others go about their duties in a responsible way and are unaffected by it. It is neither a source of great enjoyment nor an unpleasant task. But some members of Spiritual Assemblies look upon service in this capacity as a great test and sacrifice. They would much rather simply be Bahá'ís and not have to deal with the problems of administration. For them it is a drudgery, an ordeal, an unpleasant task which must be done.

Serving, in spite of personal preferences not to, is a special kind of unsung heroism. It is the price which these souls pay to free the precious, God-given institutions from those corrupting influences which have so plagued mankind in the past. When administrative authority is available to those who seek it – such as in running for office – corruption and its many ugly cousins are close at hand. When the crown of responsibility is placed upon those who do not want it, corrosive influences have little opportunity to develop.

Regardless of whether service in the institution brings pleasure, is viewed indifferently or is looked upon as a test in the path of service, it is a function which must be performed. Human society cannot exist without authority or some form of leadership.

The leadership provided by the Spiritual Assembly has many interesting features. It is true that the Spiritual Assembly must administer the affairs of the Cause, but this does not mean simply sitting back, telling other people what to do. Nor does it mean creating an administrative system beyond the needs of the community. At the present stage of development, the Universal House of Justice tells us that 'the primary purpose for which Local Spiritual Assemblies are established is to promote the teaching work' (IT viii).

All the many activities of the Spiritual Assembly reflect some aspect of leadership. In this section, six of these will be discussed: vision, inspiration, example, initiative, accessibility and credibility.

Vision

THIS CAUSE IS VERY GREAT! As leaders in the Community of the Greatest Name, Spiritual Assemblies should have, to an unsurpassed extent, a sense of destiny. The Universal House of Justice explains that 'only as individual members of Local Spiritual Assemblies deepen themselves in the fundamental verities of the Faith and in the proper application of the principles governing the operation of the Assembly will this institution grow and develop toward its full potential' (LSA, opening letter).

Members of Spiritual Assemblies, then, must strive for a better understanding of work they are doing. They must be aware of the high destiny of the Cause of God. They must look to what the institutions can become. They must see how the community can develop. This vision must be kept before the members at all times — every plan, every goal, every task performed, must be with the awareness of the high station of the institution and the community which it serves.

In making plans or goals, the Spiritual Assembly applies its vision of the future to that which the community can achieve now. This relates the grand, the lofty and the ultimate to the present. In doing this there are five steps which can be of assistance:

1. Assess the needs and the opportunities of the community.
2. Evaluate the resources available.
3. Set specific goals. These tasks or goals must be such as to challenge the community, yet be attainable.
4. Establish dates. A date for the starting of a project and a date for the completion of specific goals and tasks creates the sense of urgency necessary to produce action.
5. Design a system to check progress.

In order to be successful the Spiritual Assembly must not only establish the goals but spell out the methods by which they can be achieved. It then must guard against the two extremes of over-administration and neglect. The believers cannot function well if they feel that the Spiritual Assembly is watching every move. On the other hand, to leave committees or believers strictly on their own to secure the goals is not good leadership. It can make people feel abandoned. An atmosphere of support and loving concern is necessary. Consultation maintains the delicate balance between over- and under-administration.

Inspiration

One of the most important functions of leadership on any level is to keep hope alive. This is done by the constant attention of the Spiritual Assembly. It must convey its vision to the community and let the community know that the goals can be achieved. In reading the stories of heroes and heroines such as Quddús, Ḥujjat, Vaḥíd, Ṭáhirih and Mullá Ḥusayn, one of the most striking features is their use of speeches and exhortations to keep the believers inspired in the face of formidable obstacles. The letters from the Guardian to individual believers had one thing in common: while answering specific questions he always encouraged and renewed hope.

Be sure that the love, harmony and unity felt by members of the Spiritual Assembly is shared liberally with all the believers.

Another major challenge for the Spiritual Assembly is to be sure that everyone's talents are used:

The first quality for leadership both among individuals and Assemblies is the capacity to use the energy and competence that exists in the rank and file of its followers. Otherwise the more competent members of the group will go at a tangent and try to find elsewhere a field of work where they could use their energy.

Shoghi Effendi hopes that the Assemblies will do their utmost in planning such teaching activities that every single soul will be kept busy. (LSA 23)

Again, quoting from the Guardian: 'The best Assembly is the one that capitalizes talents of all the members of the group and keeps them busy in some form of active participation in serving the Cause and spreading the message' (USBN 11, 32, p. 3).

A valuable method of inspiring the friends is to share experiences and stories of victories won and hardships endured by others. Consultation by the Spiritual Assembly can discover many ways to achieve this worthy objective.

Example

It is extremely important that the Spiritual Assembly members be actively involved rather than passive. If the members are the example, they show true leadership. If the Spiritual Assembly members take a passive role, telling others what to do but not participating themselves, they are exercising pushership, not leadership. They must lead the way. Look at the leadership of 'Abdu'l-Bahá. One of His titles was 'the Exemplar'.

It is sometimes said that the members of the Spiritual Assembly are only members when that assembly is in session. This is only partially true. It is true for two specific functions: one is in handling personal problems; the other is in making legislative decisions. Discussion on these matters is confined to assembly consultation.

But there are other functions for which each member of a Spiritual Assembly must know that he is always an assembly member. Areas in which this is especially important are as peacemaker, making sure that love, harmony and unity prevail throughout the community at all times. Assembly members must be sure that the decisions of the assembly are carried out in a timely, effective and appropriate way. This does not mean they meddle with the jobs given others to do. They should report back to the assembly when they notice that things are not being done as directed, or unobtrusively do what they can to make sure the tasks are accomplished.

Members should also be on the alert for any information or ideas which may be useful for consultation at the next Spiritual Assembly meeting. In this way the assembly has its finger on the pulse of the community at all times.

When believers see a high degree of commitment they are encouraged. Thus, when asked to do something, they know they are not being asked to do things the Spiritual Assembly members are themselves unwilling to do. Then, when believers are faced with difficult circumstances, they know that the members of the Spiritual Assembly are completely behind them. Leadership then acquires credibility.

Initiative
Creativity and initiative cannot be summoned on command: they are gifts which appear as sparks of fire. A Spiritual Assembly must create an atmosphere of love and encouragement in which the sparks of initiative can make fire. Consultation can either fan the spark of creativity to a brilliant glow and flame or just as easily extinguish its light. Imaginative Spiritual Assemblies avoid the trap of always figuring out why things cannot be done and instead concentrate on making it possible for innovative ideas to work.

Accessibility

The believers in any community must feel that the Spiritual Assembly is available to them. The view should be that of a kind and loving parent always willing to give encouragement and a helping hand, to issue a kind word or friendly advice, or just be someone to turn to. Great care must be exercised lest there be an attitude of exclusiveness or aloofness which alienates the believers from the Spiritual Assembly. A feeling must be created that here is an institution with whom the believers are eager to share their joys and triumphs as well as their trials and woes. The confidence which this generates can produce wonderful results and creates great fortitude in times of difficulty. The believers must not abuse this condition by burdening the Spiritual Assembly with frivolous or unnecessary questions.

Credibility

The relationship between the institution and the believers should always be open, frank and loving. Since it is necessary to be obedient to the decisions of the Spiritual Assembly, it is important that too heavy a burden is not placed on the community.

Your Assembly must be very careful not to overload the Bahá'ís with rules and regulations, circulars and directions. The purpose of the administration at this time is to blow on the fire newly kindled in the hearts of these people who have accepted the Faith, to create in them the desire and capacity to teach, to facilitate the pioneer and teaching work, and help deepen the knowledge and understanding of the friends. (JWTA 67)

Several specific things can be done to strengthen the credibility of the Spiritual Assembly. Among the most important are clarity of communications, timeliness of information and reasonableness of requests made. Paying attention to these elements of leadership can go far toward strengthening the fabric of the community and making it strong, responsive and vital.

Functions of Officers

Little is said in the Bahá'í Writings about the functions of the officers of Local Spiritual Assemblies. The by-laws for incorporated Assemblies state: 'The officers of the Spiritual Assembly shall consist of a Chairman, Vice-Chairman, Secretary and Treasurer, and such other officers as may be found necessary for the proper conduct of its affairs . . .' Very little else is said about the functions of the officers.

Three observations come to mind about why so little is mentioned:
1. Any understandings we have about the functions of officers apply to this period of history only; they may or may not apply to the future.
2. While there is certain work which must be done, who does what is not important.
3. There is no inherent station in any of the offices. Other than performing certain specific services, an assembly officer is no different from any other Bahá'í.

The administrative duties of officers are described in many manuals put out by various National Spiritual Assemblies. The following comments do not deal with a list of duties; rather they are thoughts on how officers can facilitate consultation.

Chairman

The chairman, together with the secretary, is like a host and should make certain the others feel comfortable and that things run smoothly. This includes making sure that each one's contribution can flow freely with a minimum of distraction. To accomplish this the chairman should see that the physical arrangements are appropriate. Special consideration should be given to any member (such as someone in a wheelchair) who requires special attention. The chairman's attitude must be one of service. It is his responsibility to make sure meetings start and end on time. Pacing is important so that all matters receive the necessary time and attention.

At the most basic level, the chairman directs the flow of discussion, synthesizes the various contributions made, describes the gem of consensus as it emerges, identifies a trial conclusion, determines when consensus has been reached and states the decision.

During consultation the chairman has duties beyond making sure discussion is carried on in an orderly and efficient manner. He, more than anyone else, sets the tone of proper decorum and courtesy. He must make sure everyone has a chance to speak. Care must be exercised so that no one, including himself, monopolizes the discussion or intimidates others. The phrase to 'invite the reticent and quell the loquacious' has been used in this connection.

Unlike the presiding officer of most other organizations, the chairman has a duty to share his opinion. He also has the same right and responsibility to vote as any other member.

The chairman determines when consultation has been adequate. He must neither cut it short nor allow discussion to go on and on. He, or someone else appointed, should summarize the matter before a vote is taken. This statement should be clear and to the point so that everyone is sure what is being decided. If all members are clearly in agreement, voting is not necessary. However, the chairman must be sure that unanimity truly has been reached.

In general the chairman needs to have a comprehensive view of what the Spiritual Assembly is doing so that he can properly reflect its concerns. He should see priorities clearly and understand the plans, hopes and objectives of the institution. He is often the one who must analyze, synthesize, summarize and communicate the assembly's concerns both for his fellow members and to the community at large. It is his task to relate the specific actions and decisions to the major purpose.

Often the chairman is the official spokesman for the Spiritual Assembly and it is his duty to marshal the understanding and support of the entire community.

Vice-chairman

The vice-chairman serves in the absence of the chairman. This is the only specific duty assigned to him. Should the chairman die, move or resign, the vice-chairman does not automatically become the chairman; there is a new election for that position.

Secretary

Secretarial duties are many and varied. In most situations the responsibility to record and carry out the directions of the assembly falls upon the secretary. Sometimes the duties are divided between a recording or minutes secretary, corresponding secretary or assistant secretary or secretaries. Some specific functions may be assigned to some other person. The general duties are spelled out in the many administrative manuals available.

The secretary, like all other members, takes part in the discussion and votes. He is often the most familiar with the matter at hand; therefore, other members of the Spiritual Assembly are frequently dependent upon him for background information. It is important that this information be shared early in the consultation, so it is often best to have the discussion start with a background statement by the secretary.

Another important secretarial duty is maintaining the records of the Spiritual Assembly. Records are important, but the manner in which a Spiritual Assembly keeps its records and the extent of those records is a secondary issue. There are widely differing standards. A balance must be found so that adequate records are maintained for the needs of the community while guarding against too heavy a burden falling on one person or maintaining a more complex system than the needs of the community warrant. Most of all, care must be exercised that perspective is not lost. The systems of administration and record-keeping should never overshadow the purposes of teaching and building unity.

Day in and day out the secretary does all those things which need to be done to help the community function smoothly while maintaining unity. He must have patience and vision, and should project the assembly's love for the community's members, thereby ensuring that their experiences with the assembly will be as pleasant and favorable as possible. The secretary is normally the assembly's official channel of communication and should reflect the spirit and noble station of the assembly itself.

Like the chairman, the secretary must also have a firm understanding of both the general picture and the interrelationship of all Spiritual Assembly concerns.

Treasurer

In addition to his obvious duties, the treasurer should at the Nineteen Day Feast and on other occasions make the friends aware of the Fund's role in fulfilling the needs of the Faith in such an interesting and exciting manner that all will be eager to participate in contributing to it and will become aware of it as the lifeblood of the Cause. Tact is required so that contributions are made freely and without coercion or pressure. It is a challenge to keep everyone informed and stimulate eager consultation and participation without being overbearing.

These officers are usually four or more different people. In some situations it is appropriate to combine two or more of these functions. It would not be appropriate for the duties of the chairman to be combined either with that of vice-chairman or secretary. Other combinations of administrative functions may be implemented, depending on local circumstances, and other officers may be appointed or elected as necessary.

Practical Considerations

The Writings reveal a great deal about the purpose, principles, origin, nature and importance of consultation. Little is said about the details. This does not mean the details are unimportant; they must be adaptable and changed when necessary to suit the circumstances. But the principles are changeless, covering diverse situations over an incredibly long period of time.

In a letter to the National Spiritual Assembly of Iran the Guardian said that the Declaration of Trust and By-Laws '. . . are the basic and fundamental principles of the Bahá'í Community'. In addition to that, the Guardian's letters compiled in *Bahá'í Administration* are important both as a 'main source' of that Declaration and as 'a supplement to its provisions . . . these are considered as fundamental principles. What is not mentioned in them falls in the category of subsidiary matters, and diversity in such secondary questions does not at any time cause any confusion in the administration of the Cause of God' (June 2, 1934, letter from Shoghi Effendi to the National Spiritual Assembly of the Bahá'ís of Iran). 'Should there be differences and variations in secondary matters, this does not matter, because these are not regarded as basic and fundamental issues. It is indeed acceptable and desirable to have diversity in secondary matters' (Dec. 13, 1932, quoted from a letter from the Universal House of Justice to the author, May 24, 1982).

The following guidance is found in a letter to India: ' . . . the Guardian is advising that rules and regulations should not be multiplied and new statements on 'procedure' issued; we should be elastic in details and rigid in principles . . .' (DND 123).

The comparison to a building project has already been made. In building the divine edifice of the Administrative Order, local building materials must be used, adapted to the environment, requiring both local workers and methods. Secondary matters have a certain importance but they must be suited to the time, place and circumstances in which the Administration is being reared. Flexibility and diversity in these secondary matters is the only reasonable way principles can be applied to irregular and ever-changing situations.

Certain secondary matters must be decided upon for ease of consultation. In different places at different times these details will vary. That is as it should be. Here are a few items which need to be considered:

Physical setting

Knowing when, where and preferably why consultation is to take place is an obvious need. Just as important is finding a place which is reasonably comfortable and free from interruptions. Knowing how long consultation is expected to continue is also of value. Time and place should be set carefully, and once established it is best not to change. People need to be informed in time to arrange their personal affairs. Punctuality is also important. Once a meeting time is set, it is really Bahá'u'lláh's time. Treat it accordingly.

Seating

Both where people sit and the order in which they sit (and speak) can become repetitive. If everyone is accustomed to sitting in soft comfortable chairs, try sitting around a table for a change, or *vice versa*. Rearranging seating positions can also bring a little different impact to the consultation. If Charlie, the secretary, has always spoken first, followed by Jean, then Roshan, Sue, Jalil, Jim, Wilbur, Charlotte and finally Angela, the chairman, it may help to change the starting point and the order of speaking.

Agenda

Whether consultation takes place in an assembly, committee, family or a group of friends helping to solve a problem, it is important to know the topic. An agenda prepared in advance is best, and it is best if everyone can have a copy. Planning a certain amount of time for each subject is helpful. Background information is also valuable.

If an agenda has not been prepared, a review of the topics which need to be discussed is appropriate. Then decide in what order discussion will take place and how much time can be spent on each subject.

All Spiritual Assemblies, but especially those in large communities, should discuss their agendas from time to time. They should ask themselves if they are controlling the agenda or if the agenda is controlling them. Does the assembly have time to consider and accomplish what it thinks is most important or is the available time consumed in responding to items called to its attention by others?

The agenda is the accumulation of items to be discussed by the Spiritual Assembly. It must allow for those items thought of by the assembly members themselves. Is there time for creative thinking and brainstorming? devising teaching plans? study? assembly members getting to know one another better so love and harmony can flourish?

What about the responsibilities of the assembly leadership role in teaching? (not pushing or passively allowing others to teach?) promoting love and harmony? fostering the personal growth of community members?

If it appears that the agenda has taken control of the Spiritual Assembly, consult on the subject. Special committees, task forces, division of work by portfolio, staff considerations or other methods of delegation should be considered.

If the Spiritual Assembly is 'waiting to get caught up' before consulting on the agenda, it may wait a long time. As the Faith grows the work load is going to get larger and heavier. What will the Spiritual Assembly do when the community (and its problems) are twice as large? three times? ten times? one hundred times?

Varying the agenda can invigorate consultation. If the assembly has routinely jumped right into the agenda, try starting with a short study class. Change the time of the study class occasionally to the middle or end of the meeting. The order in which items are discussed could also be changed from time to time. Or devote one meeting to a single issue such as teaching. Starting with quotations on the subject to be discussed helps to get lively consultation started.

Formal versus informal discussion

Nothing in the Bahá'í Writings indicates a preference for a formal or informal style of discussion. This is apparently a detail about which believers should be elastic. In some situations formal discussion is inappropriate, in others it is highly desirable. The nature of the group and the topics being discussed should determine the degree of informality.

A relaxed, informal atmosphere can often be an aid to a free flow of ideas and creativity. It can also lead to casualness and sloppy thinking, and allow consultation to degenerate into rambling conversation. Informality works best in moderation when there is self-discipline and a sense of purpose is not lost.

In some situations, sitting in straight-backed chairs around a table is appropriate. At other times it may be impossible. Formality often reduces potential personality conflicts. The key is to be conscious of those conditions which improve the spirit of Bahá'í consultation in each specific situation and act accordingly. Changing from one arrangement to another may also help.

Expressing views

The chairman must make sure that everyone has a chance to express his own views, that no one dominates the consultation, and that all this is done with orderliness so that only one person speaks at a time. A good way to do this is to take turns speaking, e.g., the secretary might speak first, then the one to his left and so on until everyone has had an opportunity to speak on the subject, although no one should feel compelled to speak. After everyone has had a chance to say something further comments can be made. Some system can also be used to reduce the temptation for people to interrupt one another. A signal, such as a name card, can be turned to face the chairman as a request to speak.

Frequency of meeting

Whether a Spiritual Assembly meets once or twice a week or once or twice a month or irregularly is another secondary matter. The frequency of meeting is not as important as the spiritual quality of the meeting and whether or not the duties of the Spiritual Assembly are being accomplished. The question is whether or not the assembly meets often enough to fulfill its sacred obligations. Measures of this would be: are Feasts and Holy Days adequately arranged and promoted? Is teaching progressing vigorously? Does a feeling of love and unity pervade the community? Is the community life being enriched? Are child, youth and adult education receiving proper attention? Are the physical and spiritual needs of community members addressed? Is there an effective program to encourage universal participation?

These are among the obligations of the Spiritual Assembly. The frequency of meetings should be such that these items are given due attention. A balance must be maintained. It is possible to meet too often, beyond the point of effectiveness. While sacrifice is noble, no assembly member (and certainly not the whole Spiritual Assembly) should be kept on the brink of exhaustion. The strongest of bows needs to be unbent.

If meetings have been held in the same place at the same time regularly and if they tend to become dull, it may help to experiment with changing the time and place or even the length of the meeting. One assembly started meeting at 5 a.m. on Sunday morning for variety.

Motions

The use of motions in Bahá'í decision-making is strictly a secondary issue. Some National Spiritual Assemblies recommend that motions be used, and in those areas they should be. Other than that, if the Local Spiritual Assembly feels, for some reason, that motions better serve the purpose of the Assembly than a less formal means of finalizing a decision, it is free to use that method. Personally, the author discourages their use as he feels they tend to impede rather than facilitate the flow of the spirit of Bahá'í consultation.

Delegation of work

Delegation of duties is an important method for the Spiritual Assembly in the performance of all of its varied tasks. This includes work done by individuals, departments, committees, task forces, consultants, special projects, etc. The term 'committee' used here means any delegation of function to another unit. All these are agents of the Spiritual Assembly. They are extensions of that institution which carry out specific duties, and are responsible to the institution which created them. The purpose is to serve the good pleasure of the Spiritual Assembly.

The more specifically the task to be completed is defined, the easier it is for the committee to carry out the instructions. Vague directions and unclear authority are almost certain to cause frustration and a sense of failure and make an otherwise effective group of people founder in a sea of confusion. The vision must come from the Spiritual Assembly.

Whether committees are permanent or *ad hoc,* whether officers (if any) are elected or appointed, the number required to be present to carry on business are all secondary issues which the Spiritual Assembly arranges to best suit the purpose it wishes to have served.

Committee formation and functioning is a responsibility of the Spiritual Assembly which should be reviewed soon after the election at Riḍván.

There is one major area where committees are much like a Spiritual Assembly: in consultation. Consultation within a committee should be carried on in the same spirit as that described in Chapters 2 and 3. Regardless of the specific duties of the committee, it shares with the Spiritual Assembly the duty of promoting love, harmony and unity in all that it does.

Paper Assemblies

A question is sometimes raised about 'paper' assemblies. By this is generally meant those situations in which there is a Local Spiritual Assembly which does not function – that is, where the Bahá'ís do not hold assembly meetings, elections, Feasts, or do other things normally associated with a Local Spiritual Assembly. The question is, 'Why bother with these so-called assemblies which cannot even take care of their own basic responsibilities?'

The Hand of the Cause Dr Ugo Giachery was asked to what lengths a person should go to help save a non-functioning or 'paper' assembly. His reply was immediate and direct. He said, 'The Guardian said assemblies should be preserved at all costs. That means anything short of stealing, robbery or murder.' He went on to explain how often at Riḍván in Italy he would get on a train going in one direction from Rome and Angeline, his wife, would get on a train going in the other direction. They would go to communities where there were non-functioning or 'paper' assemblies, to be sure the assemblies were re-formed. It did not matter that the Bahá'ís in the area could not or would not handle the matter themselves. The assemblies had to be preserved. The level of functioning was not the issue.

As a child must be nurtured and educated, so too Spiritual Assemblies must be nurtured and educated. It is not a question of months, years or even generations. This process continues as long as necessary. But each assembly must start some time. Once continuity is lost, regaining assembly status is often very difficult.

Some Bahá'ís are culturally and/or temperamentally suited to be part of an organized community with an active Spiritual Assembly and some are not.

There is another kind of paper assembly. That is one which meets regularly but never gets beyond dealing with pieces of paper. The assembly may maintain complete minutes, hold meetings regularly and answer letters promptly. But if all it does is react to paper with other pieces of paper it may be superficial and mechanical. Record-keeping and correspondence are important, but there is no point to meetings which do nothing but create paperwork: consultation is then either heated or dull, but rarely spiritual.

Both kinds of paper assemblies – those that meet and those that do not – may be at the same level of development spiritually. The differences are that one meets and the other does not; one uses paper and the other does not.

Any assembly which is not working toward its intended purpose is a paper assembly. An assembly becomes a Spiritual Assembly when it does specific things:

1. *Promotion of teaching.* When teaching is of greatest concern and when most of the energies of the community are directed toward teaching, it may be a Spiritual Assembly rather than a paper assembly.

2. *Promoting love, harmony and unity.* An assembly may become a Spiritual Assembly when it takes deliberate steps to improve in this area.

3. *Personal growth.* When the assembly encourages the spiritual, intellectual and community life by being attentive to the following it may be a Spiritual Assembly: children receiving Bahá'í education of quality; deepening available for the adults; those in need cared for; opportunity for each community member to use his talents for the benefit of the Faith; Bahá'í fellowship extended to all.

*   *   *

Both types of paper assembly do actually exist as fully-fledged Spiritual Assemblies in the Divine World of perfection. That which is seen is only their current, beginning stage of development. Neither can be blamed or criticized for being underdeveloped any more than a child can be scolded for not growing faster. Both are alive, and therefore growth can take place.

The difference between that which is seen on the surface and that which exists in the Divine World is the potential of that Spiritual Assembly. The challenge is to move that potential from the realm of the Spirit into the temporal world. This must be done patiently and lovingly in either kind of paper assembly. Responsible institutions of the Administrative Order – Auxiliary Board members and their assistants, National Spiritual Assemblies and their appropriate committees, or Local Spiritual Assemblies given the responsibility to work with the situation – must stimulate spiritual growth from whatever stage it is at.

When Decisions are Wrong

Consultation is a *'lamp of guidance'*. It leads *'to the depths of each problem'* and makes it possible to find *'the right solution'*. It is not, however, a guarantee of infallibility; that is reserved for the Universal House of Justice. Since this is the case it must be expected that on some occasions consultation will lead to conclusions that are wrong.

One of the first things Bahá'ís should learn about the administration of the Faith is obedience to the assembly's decisions, even when that decision is wrong.

If they agree upon a subject, even though it be wrong, it is better than to disagree and be in the right, for this difference will produce the demolition of the divine foundation. Though one of the parties may be in the right and they disagree that will be the cause of a thousand wrongs, but if they agree and both parties are in the wrong, as it is in unity the truth will be revealed and the wrong made right. (BWF 411)

This clear statement implies that assemblies will sometimes make mistakes. In spite of this, some believers are not only surprised, but find it a severe test when it happens, especially when they are personally involved.

When faced with any given set of circumstances, there are usually a large number of possible actions. Most of the choices have some good features and some aspects which are not so good. The object of consultation is to come to the best possible decision using the hearts, minds, information and experience of those consulting. That would be a decision of maximum good and one least subject to error. Even when consultation is working well, it is unlikely that any assembly will come to the *only* right decision. Another group of people with the same information in the same circumstances may decide something different. That doesn't mean one decision is better than another; they may just be different. It may be a matter of taste or preference.

In the non-Bahá'í world many people look for and criticize anything with which they disagree. Criticism of elected public officials and their decisions has become common. This is sometimes followed by the decision being ignored, or by protest. Sometimes the protests become violent. The consequences of these actions ultimately lead to anarchy or revolution.

The tendency to criticize can infect Bahá'í communities too. A type of institutional backbiting can develop. Whether open or subtle it is damaging. It includes judging decisions made; comparing one

Local Spiritual Assembly or National Spiritual Assembly to another; making statements such as 'The Assembly in Lawsville is so stern and unloving while the Assembly in Lovesville is much more spiritually mature'; or 'I don't know what they're thinking of in Goofyville – they come up with the weirdest projects'; or 'The Assembly members of Successville are on an ego trip'. Statements like these violate the very spirit of the Faith.

The believers should have confidence in the directions and orders of their assembly, even though they may not be convinced of their justice or right. Once the assembly, through a majority vote of its members, comes to a decision the friends should readily obey it. Specially those dissenting members within the assembly whose opinion is contrary to that of the majority of their fellow-members should set a good example before the community by sacrificing their personal views for the sake of obeying the principle of majority vote that underlies the functioning of all Bahá'í assemblies. (LSA 26)

This puts one's loyalty to the Cause right on the line. It is no test to uphold a decision with which you agree – that is easy. Loyalty is demonstrated when you disagree and still support an action. The more strongly you disagree, the greater the need to show support and the harder you are tested.

Some people are tempted to speak out vigorously in public when they disagree. Some may even argue that it is being hypocritical not to. That is not true. Hypocrisy is a deceitful display of piety for some ulterior motive. Showing support when you disagree creates a healing atmosphere and allows time for the latent forces within the consultation to work in full possession of their Divine potential.

It is easy to say: 'If they did the right thing I would support them.' The method for the New Day functions in the reverse condition: 'I pledge my support so that they will ultimately do the right thing.' Mature faith is the understanding that in the long run upholding all decisions is best. Indeed, it is when a person most strongly disagrees with a decision, sacrifices his opinion and supports the assembly that the system of Bahá'u'lláh shines at its resplendent best.

One of the finest experiences a Bahá'í can have may come from this sacrifice of personal view. Sometimes a person has an opinion contrary to that of the majority and then he is the one given the task of carrying out the assembly decision. It may be difficult to show enthusiasm and make something work when it is contrary to a strongly-held opinion. But the experience can be extremely rewarding when the instructions are carried out in the proper spirit. When that happens the individual takes a giant leap forward spiritually and the Administration speeds toward its glorious destiny.

In contrast, a critical attitude eats away at the very basis of the spirit of the Faith. The beloved Guardian made the following statement about criticism:

Vicious criticism is indeed a calamity. But its root is lack of faith in the system of Bahá'u'lláh, i.e., the Administrative Order – and lack of obedience to Him – for He has forbidden it! If the Bahá'ís would follow the Bahá'í laws in voting, in electing, in serving and in abiding by Assembly decisions, all this waste of strength in criticizing others could be diverted into cooperation and achieving the Plan . . . (DG no. 48)

If an individual is convinced that a decision made by an assembly is wrong, he has the right to request a reconsideration. If after the reconsideration the individual still feels there is something which should be corrected, an appeal can be made to the National Spiritual Assembly through the Local Spiritual Assembly concerned. However, this request should be made lovingly, with specific arguments and reasons. A vague or general statement does no good. The point is not to challenge or confront but to request a re-examination. Once the request for reconsideration is made it is necessary to let go of the idea. Abide by and support the decision, whether or not you are convinced the action was right.

To this point the Guardian said through his secretary, 'What the Master desired to protect the friends against was continual bickering and opinionatedness. A believer can ask the Assembly why they made a certain decision and politely ask them to reconsider. But then he must leave it at that, and not go on disrupting local affairs through insisting on his own views. This applies to an Assembly member as well.' (LSA 27).

When there is support for the decision the errors will become obvious, as the Master promised. The institution can then make the necessary corrections. If met with criticism there is no way to tell whether the idea was wrong or lack of support made it unworkable. An atmosphere of criticism also tends to make differing opinions more firm and causes defensiveness to appear. Then people tend to take sides and the situation becomes worse rather than better.

If decisions are consistently wrong and the assembly seems reluctant to change, it is a severe test. It is tempting for Bahá'ís to do something else or back away from giving support. But that is when support is more important than ever. The system given by Bahá'u'lláh is self-correcting when the climate of support exists; better ideas will arise to take their rightful places. But when there is criticism and lack of support, proper growth and development are severely hampered. The situation becomes worse rather than better.

Moreover, another subtle and spiritually dangerous element creeps in. By not doing what an assembly asks, or by failing to give support, or, worse, by criticizing its decisions, the Bahá'í is really saying: 'I will obey the institutions of Bahá'u'lláh and participate only if they perform according to *my* standards and expectations.'

This creates two problems. One is the spiritual problem for the individual. The second problem is that a poisonous atmosphere is introduced into the community. Spiritual values become minimized and old-world standards reappear. The Guardian's secretary wrote on his behalf:

The Assembly may make a mistake, but, as the Master pointed out, if the Community does not abide by its decisions, or the individual Bahá'í, the result is worse, as it undermines the very institution which must be strengthened in order to uphold the principles and laws of the Faith. He tells us God will right the wrongs done. We must have confidence in this and obey our Assemblies. He therefore strongly urges you to work directly under your Bahá'í Assembly, to accept your responsibilities as a voting member, and do your utmost to create harmony within the community. (LSA 27)

Bahá'u'lláh has not given a system in which truth, justice and beauty are guaranteed in every instance. That would deny free will and would keep us from the consequences of our own mistakes. Rather, He has given a self-correcting system which gives truth, justice and beauty a better chance to develop.

In brief, support rather than the critical attitude is necessary because:

1. The Writings counsel support and forbid criticism.
2. The critical attitude is counter-productive.
3. The critical approach perpetuates the same flaws that are often a part of existing political systems.

4. The individual gains spiritually when he overcomes his natural tendency to criticize and gives support instead.

5. The community, the Cause and mankind as a whole are brought closer to that glorious day envisioned by the Master.

The Guardian's wishes in this regard are clear:

And now as I look into the future, I hope to see the friends at all times, in every land, and of every shade of thought and character, voluntarily and joyously rallying round their local and in particular their national centers of activity, upholding and promoting their interests with complete unanimity and contentment, with perfect understanding, genuine enthusiasm, and sustained vigor. This indeed is the one joy and yearning of my life, for it is the fountainhead from which all future blessings will flow, the broad foundation upon which the security of the Divine Edifice must ultimately rest. (BA 67)

SIX

Other Institutions

There are a great number of other institutions in the Faith, identified by the Guardian. Most of them are not directly involved with consultation. About a number, however, some comment should be made.

Institution of the 'Learned'

In the *Kitáb-i-'Ahdí* (the Book of His Covenant) Bahá'u'lláh wrote, 'Blessed are the rulers and the learned among the people in Al-Bahá', and referring to this very passage the beloved Guardian wrote on November 4, 1931:

In this holy cycle the 'learned' are, on the one hand, the Hands of the Cause of God, and, on the other, the teachers and diffusers of His teachings who do not rank as Hands, but who have attained an eminent position in the teaching work. As to the 'rulers' they refer to the members of the Local, National and International Houses of Justice. The duties of each of these souls will be determined in the future. (Translated from the Persian.)

The Hands of the Cause of God, the Counselors and the members of the Auxiliary Boards fall within the definition of the 'learned' given by the beloved Guardian. Thus they are all intimately interrelated and it is not incorrect to refer to the three ranks collectively as one institution.

However, each is also a separate institution in itself. (MUHJ 91–2)

The development of the assistants to the Auxiliary Board emerged after the above passage was written, but they, too, are part of the institution of the 'learned'.

Much will be written in the future about the two institutions of the rulers and the learned.* It is not my purpose here to present an analysis or description of either institution, rather the intent is to make some observations on how they relate to one another and describe some special characteristics of each institution in regard to consultation.

On April 24, 1972, the Universal House of Justice wrote a long letter which describes many features of these institutions. (It is from this letter that the above quotation was taken.) Further on in the same letter they call attention to the most striking distinction between the two, which is that 'whereas the "rulers" in the Cause function as corporate bodies, the "learned" operate primarily as individuals' (MUHJ 94).

It is this distinction which differentiates the consultation of each institution. Chapter 3 discussed collective decisions and the process used by Spiritual Assemblies. These decisions are binding, and obedience to Spiritual Assemblies is obligatory. A great deal of consultation also takes place when members of the institution of the '*learned*' are together. The actual application, however, usually takes place when members are not with their fellow members; therefore, most actions are pursued on an individual basis.

There is another important difference. Individual leadership, and recognition of the station of the learned is appropriate and encouraged. Special respect is shown to the Hands of the Cause, the Counselors, Auxiliary Board Members and their assistants. Individuals from the institution of the rulers, though, are not singled out for their contributions to the work of their Spiritual Assembly. Here the contribution which each individual makes in consultation loses its specific identity.

There are a great many other distinctions, such as the role each arm of the Administrative Order plays in the life of the Bahá'í community. To a large extent the rulers project love as that of protector, planner, leader, disciplinarian, and provider of security to the believers. The institution of the learned projects more of a love as nurturer, helper, one offering reassurance and warmth, and one to turn to when in difficulty. It is far beyond the scope of this work to go into detail on

* For further information see Eunice Braun, *The March of the Institutions: A Commentary on the Interdependence of Rulers and Learned*, George Ronald, 1984.

these differing roles. Suffice it to say their roles are different. They complement one another.

The Family

In January 1982 the Universal House of Justice published a wonderful compilation entitled *Family Life*. A covering letter refers to the family as 'an institution which is at the very base of Bahá'í society'. Bahá'u'lláh has placed the family in a most exalted position. Consider the following teachings which strengthen that basic institution:

A couple is required to know each other's *character* before marriage

Consent of the parents for marriage

Daily prayers and readings from the Writings encouraged for families

Special prayers for parents, children and spouses

Emphasis on educating children, especially the girls

Year of waiting in divorce

Maintaining the high station of the family starts with each Bahá'í's attitude toward marriage itself. A letter from the beloved Guardian describes what that attitude should be:

The Institution of marriage, as established by Bahá'u'lláh, while giving due importance to the physical aspect of marital union considers it as subordinate to the moral and spiritual purposes and functions with which it has been invested by an all-wise and loving Providence. Only when these different values are given each their due importance, and only on the basis of the subordination of the physical to the moral, and the carnal to the spiritual can such excesses and laxity in marital relations as our decadent age is so sadly witnessing be avoided, and family life be restored to its original purity, and fulfil the true function for which it has been instituted by God. (May 8, 1939, in BMFL no. 29)

No activity, no matter how important, should interfere with the well-being of the family. Not teaching. Not administrative work. There is no justification for neglecting the family. The beloved Guardian himself told the friends of this great principle; his secretary wrote on his behalf:

Surely Shoghi Effendi would like to see you and the other friends give their whole time and energy to the Cause, for we are in great need for competent workers, but the home is an institution that Bahá'u'lláh has come to strengthen and not to weaken. Many unfortunate things have happened in Bahá'í homes just for neglecting this point. Serve the Cause but also remember your duties towards your home. It is for you to find the balance and see that neither makes you neglect the other . . . (May 1929, in BMFL no. 226)

One of the truly great ways to strengthen the family is through consultation. In a letter to an individual dated August 1, 1978, the Universal House of Justice quoted the beloved Guardian as follows: 'Family consultation employing full and frank discussion, and animated by awareness of the need for moderation and balance, can be the panacea for domestic conflict' (BMFL no. 115). When plans, hopes, fears, concerns, frustrations and good news are shared, discussed and appreciated among each other potential conflicts are avoided.

Even small children can be brought into consultation in some matters. The decision, however, must rest with the parents. One Bahá'í psychologist, Dr Khalil A. Khavari, states it in this way:

Children should be granted full citizenship in the family, with its privileges and responsibilities. They should be informed about matters which affect them and gradually be incorporated as full-fledged members of the family council. Furthermore, the parents must exercise considerable wisdom in preparing items for family consultations, even as the children grow up and develop new capabilities . . .

Children should participate particularly in those decisions which directly affect them. Their participation should neither be a token involvement nor an all-consuming participation. It should be a genuine activity aimed at allowing everyone's views to be considered and reaching the soundest decision. Decisions reached by all members prevent family disunity, have greater chance for implementation, and are consistent with the ideals of love, respect, and consideration for all. (MNF 78–9)

There are, however, subjects about which the husband and wife must talk but which are best not shared with others. Examples of these might include the family budget, discipline of the children, special problems with one or more of the children, where to work, where to live, working out their own disagreements, etc. Some of these questions may be discussed in the family grouping. In general, though, the husband and wife should handle these questions in private.

The Universal House of Justice points out:

In any group, however loving the consultation, there are nevertheless points on which, from time to time, agreement cannot be reached. In a Spiritual Assembly this dilemma is resolved by a majority vote. There can, however, be no majority where only two parties are involved, as in the case of a husband and wife. There are, therefore, times when a wife should defer to her husband, and times when a husband should defer to his wife, but neither should ever unjustly dominate the other. In short, the relationship between husband and wife should be as held forth in the prayer revealed by 'Abdu'l-Bahá which is often read at Bahá'í weddings: ' Verily they are married in obedience to Thy command. Cause them to become the signs of harmony and unity till the end of time.' (BMFL no. 183)

Most marriage counselors agree that the majority of marital problems involve communication. In the close relationship between husband and wife there are bound to be misunderstandings. With the millions of items of communication exchanged, both verbal and non-verbal, sensitive spots are occasionally going to be hit. Each one learns quickly where the other is vulnerable. It is necessary to develop sensitivity and avoid those areas. Quoting again from Dr Khavari:

It is essential that the partners become inexhaustible sources of approval, assurance and acceptance. That is what marriage is all about; a private mutual admiration society. It should never deteriorate into a torture chamber where each tormentor attempts to gain the upper hand and to subdue the other. That family in which there is an abundance of assurance and approval has a most vital ingredient for the nurturance of its members. They will thrive, develop, and evolve into true human beings. They, and humanity at large, stand to reap the reward. (MNF 72)

Like other types of consultation, that between husband and wife and within the entire family is a skill, an art form, a tool for understanding which can be developed to a beautiful expression of love or allowed to deteriorate. Conscious and constant effort is required for it to flower to its full potential. When taken for granted the skill can wither and die like a flower without water.

When consultation is frank, open and loving the result is security, confidence and unity. 'Abdu'l-Bahá describes the delightful results of a family which has achieved true unity.

Note ye how easily, where unity existeth in a given family, the affairs of that family are conducted; what progress the members of that family *make, how they prosper in the world. Their concerns are in order, they enjoy comfort and tranquillity, they are secure, their position is assured, they come to be envied by all. Such a family but addeth to its stature and its lasting honour, as day succeedeth day.* (SWAB 279)

Consultation should be used to discuss matters openly, with the security of the parents retaining control. This process develops both spontaneously and during special times set aside for consultation. It is nice to have scheduled times for family conferences. This is *not* a time to lecture the children. It is a time for sharing, for planning, for uplifting. It should be full of joy and feelings of family closeness. Children learn more about consultation in this way than through any amount of study.

Informal activities are also times for consultation. Everything from mending a toy to selecting television programs or helping with family chores can be a learning experience. If the underlying attitude is one of mutual respect, love and concern, positive experiences in consultation will develop and benefits will follow naturally. Here are a few of the specific benefits:

1. It is a uniting factor. As each shares his views he is made to feel strong bonds as part of the family.

2. The most difficult problems are resolved in the warmth of those who are closest to each other.

3. When children are given an opportunity to be heard they develop the feeling that they are important and their point of view counts. They gain confidence when they speak without fear.

4. Respect for the institutions of the Faith increases because the young learn how decisions are made in the Bahá'í spirit. They watch ideas grow and their experience with this process of growth is positive.

5. When family consultation becomes natural there is a better chance that the children will automatically turn to consultation as a source of guidance during time of need. It is a protection.

6. Future generations of Bahá'ís learn this most important skill naturally and painlessly.

The Nineteen Day Feast

The Nineteen Day Feast was inaugurated by the Báb and ratified by Bahá'u'lláh in His holy book, the Aqdas, so that people may gather

*together and outwardly show fellowship and love, that the divine
mysteries may be disclosed. The object is concord, that through this
fellowship hearts may become perfectly united, and reciprocity and
mutual helpfulness be established. Because the members of the world
of humanity are unable to exist without being banded together,
cooperation and mutual helpfulness is the basis of human society. Without
the realization of these two great principles no great movement is pressed
forward . . .*

*In brief, this is my hope: that the Nineteen Day Feast become the cause
of great spiritual solidarity between the friends, that it may bring
believers into the bond of unity, and we will then be so united together
that love and wisdom will spread from this center to all parts. This Feast is
a divine Feast. It is a Lord's supper. It attracts confirmation of God like a
magnet. It is the cause of the enlightenment of hearts.* ('Abdu'l-Bahá,
quoted in BM, NDF 21)

The role of consultation in the Nineteen Day Feast is extremely
interesting. It is one of the main ways to bring these promises into
reality; it is the means through which the bond of unity is established.
All three parts of the Feast combine to produce a beautiful effect.
They are all important. To emphasize this, the Guardian wrote the
following through his secretary:

As to your question concerning Bahá'í feasts, Shoghi Effendi strongly
feels that on such occasions the friends should emphasize both the spiritual and the administrative elements. For these are equally essential to
the success of every Bahá'í festival. To maintain the right balance
between them is, therefore, the duty and responsibility of every individual Bahá'í or group. Until the believers learn to combine the two,
there can be no hope of their gaining any real and permanent benefit
from such religious celebrations. A good part of the Feast must of course
be devoted to the reading of the Holy Words. For it is through them that
the friends can get the inspiration and the vision they need for the
successful accomplishment of their work for the Cause. (BM, NDF 24)

'Abdu'l-Bahá has much to say about the Feast. He calls it '*a bringer
of joy*', '*groundwork of agreement and unity*', '*the key to affectionate
fellowship*', '*the Lord's supper*'. The Feast should be '*organized so that
the holy realities which are behind this meeting may leave behind all
prejudices and conflict, and make their hearts as a treasury of love.
Even if there is the slightest feeling between certain souls – a lack of
love – it must be made to entirely disappear. There must be the utmost
translucency and purity of intention.*' (BM, NDF 21)

It is appropriate to prepare for such an important event through prayer for its success and spending the day looking forward to it.

Upon entering the Feast keep in mind the following admonitions from the Master:

You must continue to keep the Nineteen Day Feast. It is very important; it is very good. But when you present yourselves in the meetings, before entering them, free yourselves from all that you have in your heart, free your thoughts and your minds from all else save God, and speak to your heart. That all may make this a gathering of love, make it the cause of illumination, make it a gathering of attraction of the hearts, surround this gathering with the Lights of the Supreme Concourse so that you may be gathered together with the utmost love.

O God! Dispel all those elements which are the cause of discord, and prepare for us all those things which are the cause of unity and accord! O God! Descend upon us Heavenly Fragrance and change this gathering into a gathering of Heaven! Grant to us every benefit and every food. Prepare for us the Food of Love! Give to us the Food of Knowledge! Bestow upon us the Food of Heavenly Illumination!

In your hearts remember these things, and then enter the Unity Feast.

Each one of you must think how to make happy and pleased the other members of your Assembly,* and each one must consider all those who are present as better and greater than himself, and each one must consider himself less than the rest. Know their station as high, and think of your own station as low. Should you act and live according to these behests, know verily, of a certainty, that that Feast is the Heavenly Food. That Supper is the 'Lord's Supper'! I am the Servant of that gathering. (BM, NDF 20–21)

We are at present only dimly aware of the true nature of this celebration. The second part, commonly known as the administrative or business or consultative part, will undoubtedly take on increasing importance in the lives of the Bahá'ís and the Bahá'í community in years to come.

In a dictatorship one person or a few individuals decide the affairs of the country. In a democracy it is often difficult to get people interested in civic affairs. The rule of the majority of the people is rarely expressed; decisions are made by the majority of those who take part in public affairs. Many others simply drift along in indifference.

In the Bahá'í Faith all believers take part in the affairs of the

---

* In the early days of the Faith the term 'assembly' was frequently used in the general sense to mean the Bahá'í community rather than in a strictly administrative sense.

community. This is done through the Nineteen Day Feast. The Hand of the Cause Mr Furútan referred to the Feast as the 'parliament of the future'. It is the direct link of the individual believer to all the administrative institutions of the Faith, even to the Universal House of Justice. All Bahá'ís, including children, should be encouraged to contribute to the consultation of the Feast. The result is that everyone will become involved in the affairs of the community as part of a religious celebration.

It may well be that one reason for holding the spiritual part of the Feast first is to prepare the believers spiritually for the second or administrative part. The Guardian wrote through his secretary, 'The main purpose of the Nineteen Day Feast is to enable individual believers to offer any suggestions to the local assembly which in its turn will pass it to the N.S.A.' (BM, NDF 24).

Now with reference to your last dear letter in which you had asked whether the believers have the right to openly express their criticism of any Assembly action or policy; it is not only right, but the vital responsibility of every loyal and intelligent member of the Community to offer fully and frankly, but with due respect and consideration to the authority of the Assembly, any suggestion, recommendation or criticism he conscientiously feels he should in order to improve and remedy certain existing conditions or trends in his local community, and it is the duty of the assembly also to give careful consideration to any such views submitted to them by any one of the believers. The best occasion chosen for this purpose is the Nineteen Day Feast which, besides its social and spiritual aspects, fulfills various administrative needs and requirements of the Community, chief among them being the need for open and constructive criticism and deliberation regarding the state of affairs within the local Bahá'í Community.

But again it should be stressed that all criticisms and discussions of a negative character which may result in undermining the authority of the Assembly as a body should be strictly avoided. For otherwise the order of the Cause itself will be endangered, and confusion and discord will reign in the Community. (BM, NDF 27–8)

The instruction that negative criticism should be avoided while positive recommendation encouraged seems especially illuminating. It would appear that negative matters which an individual cannot put aside by his own volition should be between that individual and the Spiritual Assembly. The entire community should not be afflicted with those criticisms which, by their nature, could undermine the Spiritual Assembly. However, everyone should be vitally involved with those things which can improve the condition of the community.

There are actually two different types of consultation carried on at the Feast, only one of which is involved with decision-making.

The second part of the Feast is the one where recommendations are made. These are forwarded to the Spiritual Assembly for its consideration. Whether or not a vote should be taken before a recommendation is forwarded to the Spiritual Assembly is a secondary matter on which the Assembly must decide (see above p. 56). In small communities, requiring a vote could result in needless waste of time and double discussion, slow down the flow of the spirit and, in fact, discourage participation and recommendations. The size and nature of the community are factors which the assembly must consider when determining whether or not it is best to vote. Once voted upon a recommendation comes from the Feast as an institution. Otherwise the Feast is a conduit or vehicle through which individual recommendations go to the assembly. The Spiritual Assembly decides which is preferable.

Either way, the recommendation from the Feast is just that: a recommendation. The assembly must consider the matter but is not bound by any recommendation from the Feast. This beautiful feature is a protection for the Cause, as popular demands may not always be in the best interest of the Faith in the long run. The duly elected Spiritual Assembly is free to make the final decision without coercion.

The other type of consultation during the Feast is for insight and understanding. It produces greater strength in the Covenant even though no decisions or recommendations result. This is when the friends consult on different topics for better understanding and/or personal resolve.

In the third part of the Feast there is a splendid opportunity to weave the social fabric of the Bahá'í community. This should maintain the high spiritual level of the other parts. Consultation may continue during this time. However, it will generally be among groups of two, three or four believers discussing some item of special interest to them. If this is carried on with the spiritual concern for fostering love and unity, getting clarification or better understanding of something, or for solving a particular problem, it can become a delightful, beneficial and inspirational form of consultation.

The Fund

The institution of the Bahá'í Fund finds its way into practically every undertaking of the Faith. It is a highly appropriate topic for consultation in three different ways.

Importance

The importance of the Fund makes it an urgent matter for discussion both within the institutions of the Faith and among the believers generally. The beloved Guardian referred to it as '. . . the prerequisite of future progress and achievement' (LBC 4, May 25, 1926), 'the bedrock on which all other institutions must necessarily rest and be established . . . the life-blood of those nascent institutions . . . (LBC 9, July 29, 1935).

These comments from the Guardian suggest that consultation is appropriate to make certain all believers are aware of its importance. Just exactly what is meant by the Fund as a prerequisite? bedrock? lifeblood?

Contributions

Beyond the obvious need for money, consultation is a way to let all believers be aware of the privilege of participating in the Fund. Why are contributions not accepted from those who are not registered Bahá'ís? What is the spiritual basis of giving? Why does the removal of membership rights include forfeiting the privilege of contributing to the Fund? How can each community fulfill the Guardian's request for '. . . the whole-hearted, the ever-increasing and universal support of the mass of believers . . .'? (LBC 14, August 8, 1957)

These are just a few of the areas of concern about the Fund which require consultation both for understanding and practical reasons. Consultation on these subjects should not be limited to Spiritual Assemblies. Rather, the topic is of general, constant concern and even appropriate for informal settings.

Disbursements

There are few topics which Spiritual Assemblies find more challenging than how to use their limited funds. The Guardian anticipated this concern early in his ministry when he said, '. . . strongly urge, nay entreat, the friends not to dissipate their efforts, but to seek, after frank, mature and continuous deliberation, to arrive at a common conclusion as to the most urgent requirements and needs of the hour . . .' (BA 77).

He talked about 'limitations of our resources' (BA 183) and encouraged the believers to '. . . study the needs of the Cause, find the fields which will give the greatest yield and then appropriate the necessary funds. And such a task is surely most difficult and responsible' (LBC 15).

This can be done with careful consultation. What is required is a review of priorities for those limited resources. Even the idea of the 'greatest yield' needs discussion in the light of ever-changing circumstances. It is no easy task, as anyone who has compared the needs with the limited money available knows. Sometimes there are no simple answers. When considerations are made, the Spiritual Assembly is really reviewing its priorities. It is a hard discipline to keep priorities in order; but the tool of consultation is equal to that challenge.

Summer Schools

The beloved Guardian stated that summer schools play an important part in 'the steady development of local Bahá'í community life [which] . . . is the bedrock of Bahá'í national growth and development' (CBL no. 4), and bring 'forth jewels from the mine of humanity . . .' (CBL no. 1).

Consultation is important for a successful Summer School in two different ways. One has to do with arranging the school for the harmonious combination of 'the threefold features of devotion, study and recreation' (CBL no. 7) and is carried out by those who are responsible for its administration.

The other use of consultation is in the school itself. There is no better place to experience Bahá'u'lláh's promises about what can be gained by the individual from consultation.

The Guardian stressed study and 'a thorough discussion, both formally and informally, of various aspects of the Cause' (CBL no. 34). This is neither more nor less than consultation, scheduled and spontaneous, as a part of classes or during more relaxed periods to allow the benefits of the school to sink deeply into the hearts of all attending.

The object should be to develop a thirst 'that will stimulate the students to proceed in their studies privately once they return home . . .' (CBL no. 20).

Conventions

Conventions, both national and those for electing delegates, provide some of the most intense periods of consultation for many Bahá'ís. The same principles of spiritual consultation apply in Conventions as in other circumstances. There are, however, some items which make this experience unique.

Consultation at the Convention has a threefold purpose:
a. For all those attending to learn the current conditions, problems and possibilities of the Faith.
b. For the delegates to make constructive suggestions to the incoming National Spiritual Assembly.
c. For all to contribute to and benefit from the unity in spirit and action of the entire community.

Obviously, consultation is an integral part of the proceedings on the Convention floor. Details, such as the manner of making recommendations, vary, but the basic principles of consultation must be very much in evidence for the proper spirit to be present.

In the corridors, between the sessions, during meals, there is another extremely important form of consultation taking place. Friends gather to talk and consult about many things. This is when individual plans develop. Teaching projects, pioneering plans, other enterprises for the benefit of the Cause spring from the spontaneous exchange of the friends, the informal consultation during this annual festive occasion.

There is probably no time during the year that witnesses a greater burst of creative ideas and energy. It is surely occasions such as these which 'Abdu'l-Bahá may have had in mind when He said: *'Such consultation causeth the living waters to flow in the meadows of man's reality, the rays of ancient glory to shine upon him, and the tree of his being to be adorned with wondrous fruit'* (CC no. 15).

The fruits of the tree of consultation from Conventions have provided nutritious results for the entire planet. So many victories for the Faith, on both a grand and a modest scale, can be traced to chance remarks between two lovers of Bahá'u'lláh during their own private consultation at a Convention.

SEVEN

Weaving the Social Fabric

In the new civilization created by the Pen of Bahá'u'lláh, social activity takes on new dimensions. The Revelation ennobles the human spirit and produces a greater fulfillment of man's potential. Mighty institutions, unlike any created in the past, are reared, enabling humanity to forge ahead into its exciting future. They are a bulwark against the problems of life – problems both great and small.

There is also a delightful re-creation of the social life, clothing mankind in an exquisite new spiritual garment. Consider these teachings:

The prohibition of backbiting, gossip and slander

The elimination of prejudices

Universal language, script, education, currency, systems of weights and measures

The elimination of the extremes of wealth and poverty

These are just a few of the many principles designed to improve personal and business relationships, fitting mankind out in its new and wondrous robe.

Consultation weaves the fabric of this Bahá'í society. Whether believers are trying to understand the meanings of the Creative Word, conferring within an institution, planning a teaching project, helping one another in personal matters, having a party, taking children on a picnic, trying to beautify their own surroundings, or simply pursuing leisure-time activities, consultation may be a part of it. When there is love, unity and harmony, and when there is sharing of thoughts, feelings and points of view, allowing new ideas to emerge, there is consultation.

In this weaving of the social fabric, one might liken the mighty institutions, the laws and principles given by the Supreme Manifestation, to the warp – the strings of a loom that stand up and down. They are held firmly in place by the strength of the Covenant. Through the warp runs the woof – the sideways or horizontal threads. These are the personalities, strengths and weaknesses, charms and quirks of the individual believers woven among the laws, principles and institutions to create the fabric of the new society.

Consultation is the shuttle which pulls the threads of our individual personalities through the secure, well-placed strings of the warp. The whole pattern of humanity is woven in all its color, divine splendor and artistry to reflect the genius and brilliance of the new day as envisioned by the Supreme Manifestation of God.

In this way even tangled, frayed and unruly strands of personality become blended into the pattern of Bahá'í society. Without the shuttle of consultation, the blending of the diverse elements of humankind into a strong and beautiful tapestry would be impossible.

Much of the weaving goes on in the everyday, routine events of life. Even ordinary conversation can be elevated to consultation when the attitude is one of sharing and the proper spirit is maintained. Spontaneous and incidental consultation contributes to the mighty process of weaving the social fabric. Here are a few examples:

Deepening

The benefit of 'illumination' from consultation is probably more clearly demonstrated in deepening activities than at any other time.

Consultation bestoweth greater awareness and transmuteth conjecture into certitude. It is a shining light which, in a dark world, leadeth the way and guideth. For everything there is and will continue to be a station of perfection and maturity. The maturity of the gift of understanding is made manifest through consultation. (CC no. 3)

Several things happen simultaneously when Bahá'ís use consultation for deepening. First of all, new information is gained. Second, new insights are found and understandings clarified. These help to relate facts to each other better, making the information more valuable and useful. This is illumination. Third, a bond is formed. Bahá'ís who consult with each other about the teachings develop a closeness that is especially precious. Fourth, strength is gained to face new opportunities or difficult problems. Often the means of dealing with them also become clear. Fifth, as *'conjecture'* changes into *'certitude'* a quality of assurance develops which affects every facet of the individual's life. One becomes more assured, oriented and fundamentally happy. Sixth, and most important of all, is the consolidation of belief. This draws us closer to our Maker, helping us to know and worship Him, which is, of course, the object of life.

These things happen whether there is a formal study class or informal discussion. During the social part of the Nineteen Day Feast, during Conventions, conferences, schools, while visiting neighbors, and in many other circumstances there can be consultation with these results. Consultation exists whenever the attitude and subject are right. Through this form of consultation souls are woven into the fabric of the Cause, enriching both the individuals concerned and the Bahá'í community.

Teaching

Some Bahá'ís are surprised to learn that one of the main reasons Spiritual Assemblies were established was to further the teaching work. As early as 1926 the beloved Guardian wrote:

As the administrative work of the Cause steadily expands, as its various branches grow in importance and number, it is absolutely necessary that we bear in mind this fundamental fact that all these administrative activities, however harmoniously and efficiently conducted, are but means to an end, and should be regarded as direct instruments for the propagation of the Bahá'í Faith. (BA 103)

In a letter to Australia and New Zealand the Guardian wrote, through his secretary, '. . . one of the reasons for so painstakingly building up Assemblies is for them to promulgate the Cause of God . . .' (LGANZ 68–9). In the last year of his life the Guardian stated this even more strongly: 'The paramount task is, of course, the teaching work; at every session your assembly should give it close attention, considering everything else of secondary importance' (SML 19, July 28, 1957).

However, these instructions were never intended to take away the individual's responsibility. Teaching remains primarily a personal obligation. Speaking of the goals of the first Seven Year Plan the beloved Guardian gave this reminder:

It is the bounden duty of every American believer . . . to initiate, promote and consolidate . . . any activity he or she deems fit to undertake for the furtherance of the Plan . . . Let him not wait for any directions, or expect any special encouragement, from the elected representatives of his community . . . [on] his own initiative . . . [let him resolve] to arise and respond to the call of teaching . . . (ADJ 42)

While it is the duty of the Spiritual Assembly to attempt to keep everyone involved, it is the even greater duty of the individual to arise to serve, even when there is no special encouragement from the institutions.

The importance of teaching cannot be overstated. The Ancient Beauty equated teaching His Cause with martyrdom. It is one of the two things which are pleasing in the sight of God (RBii 94). This is interesting to think about. While many of the martyrs go joyously and confidently to win their crown of victory, there are probably a great many others who are frightened or do not feel worthy. They have been caught in circumstances over which they had little control and have been forced to surrender their lifeblood – the supreme act of devotion. We, today, are caught in countless circumstances over which we have little control and we join ranks with the martyrs by teaching – this supreme act of devotion even though we too may feel frightened and unworthy and would rather serve in some other manner.

In addition, the Master was even more specific when He said, '*In this day every believer must concentrate his thoughts on teaching the Faith . . . O loved ones of God! Each one of the friends must teach at least one soul each year. This is everlasting glory. This is eternal grace*' (IT no. 30).

There are two extremely important things to be done regularly in order to achieve this goal.

1. Pray diligently daily to be led to those who are receptive. The more urgent and intense the prayer, the greater the chance of success.
2. Consult with others about it. The consultation should center around both individual activities and how two or more can work together to fulfill that mandate from 'Abdu'l-Bahá.

A myriad questions will still arise. How should I get started? Should I be direct or indirect? The Writings state that teaching must be done with 'wisdom'. What is 'teaching with wisdom'? Whom shall I approach? How shall I approach them? How do I know when I have found a receptive soul? What is the best piece of literature to give out? What if I say the wrong thing? How can I bring up the Faith? I'm really too shy, isn't there some other way to get this done? I don't know enough to teach. What if I make a mistake? I'm not 'spiritual' enough. Why should I do it? Let someone else. These and countless other questions flood the minds and hearts of many Bahá'ís. For some teaching is easy and natural. For others it is not.

In consultation Bahá'u'lláh has given us a means to remove the fears, doubts and questions which arise about teaching, and also to provide the stimulus, motivation and enthusiasm to accomplish this essential work. When believers talk about teaching, exciting things start to happen. In talking with one's spouse, one's children or other Bahá'ís – in person, by telephone or letter – one can consult about teaching. As this goes on ideas for teaching are generated. The Guardian assures us, 'With proper consultation some method is sure to be found. There is no need to wait until an Assembly is constituted to start consulting. The view of two earnest souls is always better than one' (CC no. 30).

A good time to start consulting on teaching is now. Make some plans. Plans for individual teaching can be discussed with someone else, or even by consulting your own mind and heart. Making group teaching plans for a family, a neighborhood, or collection of friends, or a plan for traveling teaching, is a wonderful experience. Plans, of course, are only good if they are carried out: there must be a system for follow-up. Plans are the preparation for teaching, not a substitute for it.

There are many beautiful stories of pioneers from Africa, South America, the Pacific – all over. The pioneers had been at a dead end. No matter what they did they could make no progress. Then, in consultation with a spouse, a travel teacher, other pioneers, or through consultation by correspondence, some new insight was found. An idea or approach became apparent and the whole project was changed as avenues opened up.

One of the most refreshing and exciting of Bahá'í activities is to review teaching experiences with family and friends, at the Feast or on other occasions. This does three things:

1. The exchange of ideas helps everyone learn new methods from each other.
2. In discussing teaching experiences (successes and failures) we learn how to improve.

3. There is no greater stimulus and encouragement for each other than the sharing of experiences. Enthusiasm breeds more enthusiasm, which is vital for teaching. Some communities make the sharing of teaching experiences a regular feature of the social part of their Nineteen Day Feasts.

One of the most overlooked values of consultation is as a teaching tool itself. Bahá'ís, practised in the art of consultation, have developed skills of speaking, listening and cooperating which are not common. The Master said,

The friends of God should weave bonds of fellowship with others and show absolute love and affection towards them. These links have a deep influence on people and they will listen. When the friends sense receptivity to the Word of God, they should deliver the Message with wisdom. They must first try and remove any apprehensions in the people they teach. In fact, every one of the believers should choose one person every year and try to establish ties of friendship with him, so that all his fear would disappear. Only then, and gradually, must he teach that person. This is the best method. (IT no. 27)

This statement suggests some interesting ideas. How many people have heard of the Cause because they were asked something first? Countless pioneers have endeared themselves to the people, won friends for the Faith and enlisted new believers because they arrived fully armed with ignorance and in honest humility asked advice about everything, from the location of the Post Office to questions of basic survival. Bahá'ís who learn the skill of consultation have the most useful tool in the world to weave those very bonds of fellowship of which 'Abdu'l-Bahá speaks.

Consultation and teaching indeed are an ideal couple. Consultation should be used in making plans, carrying out those plans and, afterwards, sharing the experience with others. It should be used in searching our own hearts, souls and consciences, with family and friends, in groups and in assemblies, and, as a teaching tool, with those with whom we wish to share this precious Message.

Informal Settings

Recreation
It is a special joy when believers find recreational activities they can share. Sewing, sports, music, art or handicrafts can all contribute to

the weaving of the fabric of Bahá'í society. The more activities Bahá'ís share with one another the better. Making necessary plans for a fishing trip or planning a musical event, or whatever, provide opportunities for the shuttle of consultation.

Work projects

Another excellent opportunity for weaving the new civilization is when Bahá'ís work with one another. It is wonderful when believers work together in specific service to the Cause. It is also nice when they help each other in strictly personal matters. The benefit comes from the additional work which is accomplished and the enjoyment of being together; consultation enriches the experience, and the result is much greater than it would be with each working separately.

Bahá'í group

In any community where there is no Local Spiritual Assembly a group should be formed. Within the group the Bahá'ís function much as an assembly would. There are the benefits of collective wisdom and working together. However, the group has no authority to conduct Bahá'í marriages or handle personal problems or other administrative matters which require an institution. A group cannot act in any legal capacity.

Sometimes, even where there is a Local Spiritual Assembly, it cannot function because it is not possible to get a quorum together. The work of the Cause cannot be allowed to stand still because of this inconvenience. Those who can get together should work as a group to be sure that the teaching work continues, and that children's classes, deepenings and Feasts are arranged. Any plans made can be changed or confirmed by the Local Spiritual Assembly once it is possible to get a quorum again. Consultation can thus continue even when conditions are less than ideal.

*   *   *

In brief, the benefits of consultation can be found in any situation; the more this shuttle is used, the better the fabric of Bahá'í society will be. Practising consultation in informal situations also helps to develop that skill for use in the institutions. This produces a natural, comfortable and harmonious link between the everyday affairs of life and the administrative needs of the divine society.

Business and Professional Affairs

The Center of the Covenant was once asked a question the answer to which put the whole matter of commercial enterprise in an interesting light:

Regarding thy question about consultation of a father with his son, or a son with his father, in matters of trade and commerce, consultation is one of the fundamental elements of the foundation of the Law of God. Such consultation is assuredly acceptable, whether between father and son or with others. There is nothing better than this. Man must consult in all things for this will lead him to the depths of each problem and enable him to find the right solution. (CC no. 18)

Further to this point, the Guardian quotes 'Abdu'l-Bahá as saying:

The purpose of consultation is to show that the views of several individuals are assuredly preferable to one man, even as the power of a number of men is of course greater than the power of one man. Thus consultation is acceptable in the presence of the Almighty, and hath been enjoined upon the believers, so that they may confer upon ordinary and personal matters, as well as on affairs which are general in nature and universal.

For instance, when a man hath a project to accomplish, should he consult with some of his brethren, that which is agreeable will of course be investigated and unveiled to his eyes, and the truth will be disclosed. Likewise on a higher level, should the people of a village consult one another about their affairs, the right solution will certainly be revealed. In like manner, the members of each profession, such as in industry, should consult, and those in commerce should similarly consult on business affairs. In short, consultation is desirable and acceptable in all things and on all issues. (CC no. 17)

These statements from the Master have fascinating implications so far as the business and professional lives of Bahá'ís are concerned. The fact that people happen to be Bahá'ís is no reason why they should be in business or professional ventures together; on the other hand, there is no reason why they should not be. If there is common interest, believers can benefit from consultation with one another, even with those who are not working in the same field.

There are two quite different elements in business and professional situations in which consultation can play an important role. One is the field of abstract ideas and the other has to do with practical matters.

Abstract ideas

One of the truly delightful qualities in human beings is the pleasure derived from talking about things remote. Speculation on the future, the exchanging of ideas or the exploring of new thoughts are exhilarating to many. Whenever people with common interests gather together conversation will reflect that interest. That is wonderful! Chances are that if three women in the advanced stages of pregnancy happen to meet, sooner or later the conversation will be about the new lives growing in their respective wombs. Plans, dreams, hopes and fears will be expressed – all of which spring from their common condition.

Mankind has benefited greatly from the abstract and 'dreamy' remarks of those with similar interests talking or speculating about things not related to the present.

In His prayer revealed for the Southern States 'Abdu'l-Bahá writes of '. . . *Thy confirmations, which alone can change a gnat into an eagle, a drop of water into rivers and seas, and an atom into lights and suns?* (TDP 68). Imagine some Bahá'ís interested in physics talking about that passage. The power which has been made manifest through the atom is compared to the sun. We already know of the awesome power – for good or for evil – which the atom can release. The same reasoning applies to the drop in relationship to the sea. One can speculate about the amount of energy which would be available when the scientists of the future unlock the power of a molecule of water.

At the present time that is an abstraction. Yet Bahá'ís interested in physics and interested in speculating may get a lot of enjoyment from discussing something like this. Eventually some scientist might speculate on some chance remark from this consultation and be led to a discovery of enormous benefit to mankind. The seed would be in the prayer of 'Abdu'l-Bahá. Germination comes from the abstract consultation.

The principle is that through consultation those with common interests are able to focus their thoughts. A new power is generated which can be used in whatever direction it is turned. Affairs of business, science, housekeeping, recreation, can all benefit from this type of exchange.

Practical matters

Many fields in the business or professional worlds, in the trades, in commerce or in the arts could benefit from the use of consultation as a practical tool. The Master foresaw this when He said:

The question of consultation is of the utmost importance, and is one of the most potent instruments conducive to the tranquillity and felicity of the people. For example, when a believer is uncertain about his affairs, or when he seeketh to pursue a project or trade, the friends should gather together and devise a solution for him. He, in his turn, should act accordingly. Likewise in larger issues, when a problem ariseth, or a difficulty occurreth, the wise should gather, consult, and devise a solution. They should then rely upon the One true God, and surrender to His Providence, in whatever way it may be revealed, for divine confirmations will undoubtedly assist. Consultation, therefore, is one of the explicit ordinances of the Lord of mankind. (CC no. 14)

In the artistic world, how much inspiration has been born and brought to fruition as a result of consultation in the sense of sharing!

Even the writing of this book would have been impossible were it not for the loving consultation of friends in person, by telephone and by correspondence. This consultation helped clarify thoughts, refine thinking and cast ideas in new and different lights. For the author it was a marvelous example of the benefits the Center of the Covenant described.

In any field a time comes to try the untried. Before marching into the unknown it can be helpful to seek the wise counsel of those whose judgments are respected. Taking trusted friends into one's confidence in consultation can be highly rewarding.

Sooner or later most people find themselves up against difficult decisions which must be faced in connection with their work. When there is a resource of caring people in whom to confide in order to help make these decisions, that is naturally an advantage. It is appropriate to call several people together to discuss the problem and to help get one's own thinking clarified. The others are not necessarily being asked to make the decision, but to help identify the real issues and clarify the situation. This gives illumined understanding, so that difficult decisions can be made with greater wisdom and conviction.

One of the most important parts of any business is evaluation. Is the daily activity really contributing toward the objective of the business? In other words, is that which is desired really being accomplished? Much money is spent on such things as financial statements, profit and loss statements, consultants and other means of getting an evaluation. Once the information is assembled, the next step is understanding the data and its implications. There is a huge untapped source of assistance available. Whether or not people are in the same business, those with experience of responsible decision-making can certainly give a great deal of help in reviewing the data and consulting about it. The insights gained can be at least as valuable as the data itself.

Some people may be reluctant to enter into such a process because they may feel vulnerable, and no one wants to expose his vulnerability. Or they may feel they are imposing on other Bahá'ís. In the critical and judging society in which we live much effort is expended on putting up one's guard to avoid having others know too much about one's own affairs. If this feeling of vulnerability is overcome and one is willing to expose himself to the examination of friends and colleagues in the atmosphere of consultation, enormous benefit can result. It also benefits those asked to consult.

Wherever there are people there are bound to be disputes. The Guardian has specifically discouraged Bahá'ís from using the civil courts in settling disagreements. Instead, problems can be resolved in several ways:

1. The individuals may talk out their problems and come to an amicable agreement.

2. The matter can be referred to a Local Spiritual Assembly. There is, however, no obligation to take it to the Local Spiritual Assembly and the assembly may choose not to become involved.

3. Asking assistance from an Auxiliary Board member or assistant may prove helpful. Their function is not to arbitrate the dispute, but they can render enormous service in placing the issues in their proper perspective and helping the disputing parties work out their problems. They may also be able to advise when a matter should be referred to the other branch of the Administrative Order.

4. Another means is to select trusted Bahá'ís who are not involved and ask them to consult on the issues. While the results of this would not be legally binding, there is a great benefit in that it may well avoid potential difficulties and hard feelings. It certainly is far better than going to court. Obviously, if all other measures fail and matters cannot be resolved, it may be necessary to use the civil courts.

The sooner assistance is requested in resolving a dispute, the better. When relationships have been allowed to deteriorate into hard feelings and the fixing of blame it may be difficult to bring about a healing.

These are just some of the uses of consultation which are available to businesses, the professions, the trades, the arts, commercial and other enterprises. The more Bahá'ís consciously enter into consultation in all their affairs, the better.

The Non-Bahá'í World

Once the marvels available through consultation have been discovered there is a natural and exuberant desire to use it for everything. Unfortunately, it does not work in some non-Bahá'í circumstances. Yet there are general principles which can be applied outside the Faith.

Some of the reasons why the principles of consultation do not transfer completely are as follows:

1. Without the spirit, love, harmony and unity there is no consultation. The quality of the love implied is related to Divine love – in which each sees in the other the reflection of the spirit of Bahá'u'lláh. In other words, if the common acceptance of Bahá'u'lláh is not there, the conditions which allow consultation to function at its best may not be present.

2. A prime requisite for those who take counsel together is purity of motive. It is extremely difficult for people to put aside their own personal or private interests for the benefit of the whole. Most people have personal motives or a limited point of view which play heavily in all decisions. In Bahá'í consultation there is a deliberate effort to make these limitations gradually disappear. More typical in other settings is the tendency to promote one's own views unless compromise becomes expedient.

3. Bahá'í consultation must be for a purpose such as solving a problem, making some plans, or getting a better understanding of something. It is all too easy for discussion to become rambling and misdirected, thereby losing its intent. It takes practice and patience to keep one's thinking on the objective to the end. Bahá'ís get this training in consultation.

There are, however, some qualities developed, some disciplines and skills learnt in consultation, which are extremely useful in other situations. Bahá'ís often use these without being aware of it. Among them are:

1. *The ability to listen effectively.* This quality is so rare in the world that Bahá'ís who learn this in consultation find themselves well regarded because of it. They are able to help others because of their creative listening.

2. *Pursuit of excellence.* In serving the Faith, Bahá'ís seek situations which are in the best interests of the Cause. They frequently make great sacrifices, learning to give up the important to the most important, to set priorities. This discipline can carry over into other areas.

3. *Attitude.* A positive attitude develops from consultation. This attitude is useful everywhere: the positive approach can help reorient an entire group. Frequently, believers have been surprised by the impact their presence has made. Colleagues often say they feel better just because a certain individual is present.

4. *Action.* Bahá'ís are not simply decision-makers expecting someone else to carry out the orders. They have the habit of being involved in whatever they decide because of their training through consultation.

5. *Leadership.* In the Bahá'í community leadership is very real, but different. Rather than leadership surrounding a charismatic or promising personality, it generally comes from the quality of the peace-maker. True leadership is being able to infuse spirit and direction into a group. Bahá'ís tend to develop that quality unconsciously. In other circumstances they easily assume a leadership role without being authoritarian. This is a rare and needed quality in the world.

Bahá'ís also develop the ability to follow without being servile. Once again, they are trained to work together for the benefit of the whole.

6. *Problem-solving.* Techniques for problem-solving discussed elsewhere (see Chapters 10 and 13) frequently provide a refreshing approach to issues needing to be resolved in non-Bahá'í settings.

While these things are not the purpose of consultation, they are valuable qualities. So, although the principles of consultation cannot be directly transferred to all non-Bahá'í settings, many of the benefits learnt in consultation can be applied to other situations. The whole world is richer as a result.

EIGHT

Individual Differences and Consultation

Just as no two snowflakes are alike, so no two human beings are the same. Even identical twins are different – physically, in their personalities and their characters. The uniqueness of every person is an attraction, a challenge, and a vital part of consultation.

Differences, by their very nature, tend to divide people. But through the power of the Covenant and the method of consultation the Ancient Beauty has taken points of difference and forged them into a source of strength.

There is a comparison in music. Different notes, sounded at random, can produce an awful noise; yet those same notes, when arranged to harmonize with each other, produce beautiful music. When the differences among people are harmonized those results, too, can be lovely. When allowed to clash the results can be terrible.

Through consultation the complex issues of the modern day can be better understood because different points of view, discussed under a spiritual discipline, result in a more complete view of the situation. With the searchlight of consultation a special illumination is produced. When functioning at its harmonious best consultation enables the differences among people to combine, producing reasonable and practical solutions even when the problems are difficult and involved.

This chapter examines some of these individual differences. While attention is drawn to the variations which exist among people emphasis is laid on the transforming of discord into the creative energy of unity.

The True Self

Among the most puzzling questions of life are those concerning the self. What is self? What is the true self? Is the self a single thing or is it a complex interaction of separate and distinct parts? These questions have been pondered through the ages and in modern times subjected to extensive research using elaborate techniques and sophisticated computer analysis. Many theoretical explanations have been suggested, but all of them seem to leave unanswered questions.

It is safe to say that the self does have interacting elements which are constantly changing. It seems separate, yet whole; subtle, yet manifest; sometimes a well-integrated unit and sometimes a mass of conflict and confusion. In common speech we say, 'pull yourself together', or 'he is beside himself'. During moments of indecision we say, 'part of me says "yes" and part of me says "no"', or 'I had to have a stern talk with myself about that'. A well-integrated person is one who is mentally healthy and not 'coming apart'.

While the various aspects of the self may not be distinctly separate parts, it is helpful to look at some of the different elements. The Bahá'í Writings are a mine of information about these characteristics.

Spirit

'Abdu'l-Bahá spoke of five categories of spirit (SAQ 208). Two of these, the animal spirit and the human spirit, relate to the sense of self.

The *animal spirit* pertains to our physical being, including *'the power of all the senses'* (SAQ 208). Creature needs are a part of life. We eat, sleep, breathe, live and die according to their dictates. Man functions biologically in a manner similar to the animal kingdom, which is why experiments with animals have proved beneficial in many ways.

Beyond the animal spirit is the *human spirit 'which distinguishes man from the animal'* (SAQ 208). A major difference between them is that *'The animal is the captive of the senses and bound by them . . .'* (SAQ 188), whereas the human spirit can be freed from some animal restraints. Yet there is no basic conflict between the animal spirit and the human. 'Abdu'l-Bahá referred to the animal force in man as a *'partner'* (PT 17). In fact, the human spirit has enormous potential for either good or evil. *'How lofty is the station which man, if he but choose to fulfill his high destiny, can attain! To what depths of degradation he can sink, depths which the meanest of creatures have never reached'* (GL 206).

Some people are slaves to their animal natures. Their biological functions, drives and needs consume their thoughts and direct their every action. Many people, on the other hand, are liberated from the domination of the physical of self. They control their animal appetites and their bodies become worthy temples for their souls.

Dual nature of man

The Master had this to say about these two possibilities which are aspects of the human spirit:

In man there are two natures; his spiritual or higher nature and his material or lower nature. In one he approaches God, in the other he lives for the world alone. Signs of both these natures are to be found in men. In his material aspect he expresses untruth, cruelty and injustice; all these are the outcome of his lower nature. The attributes of his Divine nature are shown forth in love, mercy, kindness, truth and justice, one and all being expressions of his higher nature. Every good habit, every noble quality belongs to man's spiritual nature, whereas all his imperfections and sinful actions are born of his material nature. If a man's Divine nature dominates his human nature, we have a saint.

Man has the power both to do good and to do evil; if his power for good predominates and his inclinations to do wrong are conquered, then man in truth may be called a saint. But if, on the contrary, he rejects the things of God and allows his evil passions to conquer him, then he is no better than a mere animal. (PT 60)

This takes us to the very heart of humanness: a constant struggle between man's lower nature and his higher one. One tradition speaks of the 'black dog' and the 'white dog' within each person. Robert Louis Stevenson wrote a famous novel about Dr Jekyll and Mr Hyde. Dr Jekyll was a very good man who, when he drank a certain drug, became Mr Hyde, an unbelievably cruel person. Both dwelt in the same body. Each of us has some of Dr Jekyll and Mr Hyde within us.

THE LOWER SELF. This aspect of the human spirit has also been called the material nature. Tendencies to evil have been described throughout the ages as the devil, Satan, the evil whisperer, Beelzebub, the forces of darkness and so on. The Center of the Covenant reveals the true identity of this demon when He says: '. . . *the evil spirit, Satan or whatever is interpreted as evil, refers to the lower nature in man'* (PUP 294). When someone says that something is the work of the devil, it is from that lower nature. In the *Ishraqát* Bahá'u'lláh refers to this self as hell (TB 118). The beloved Guardian referred to this as '. . .

the ego,* the dark, animalistic heritage each one of us has, the lower nature that can develop into a monster of selfishness, brutality, lust and so on' (LL 28, December 1947).

Self-interest, reflected in the ego, made survival possible during man's more primitive stages. However, this crude self-centeredness becomes the cause of much anguish in modern man. As a source of evil it acts in different ways for different people. For some it is a distorted sense of importance, a prideful attitude, boastfulness, arrogance and a great need for recognition and attention. Others have a lower sense of self-worth. False humility, excessive timidity and self-defeating activities are also part of this ego problem.

A common expression of ego is an excessive self-referencing that expresses itself in a tendency to focus every conversation on one's own experiences and concerns. Despair, officiousness, self-pity, depression, self-aggrandizement, defensiveness, bitterness or hostility come easily to anyone with exaggerated self-concern.

Another aspect is cruelty and malevolence. When the lower nature is in command, there may be a desire to subdue or even destroy anyone who is perceived to be a threat, or against whom there is jealousy or ill-feeling. One literally becomes an 'instrument of the devil', that is, of his lower nature.

When the appetites of the lower nature get out of control one becomes a captive of his vices. The iron grip of sexual perversions, greed, gambling, quest for power, alcohol or other chemical dependences can be utterly devastating. Virtually nothing can deter someone in pursuit of these all-consuming vices.

Pleasure-seeking can also become the object of impassioned determination. Even games can become extremely serious business with which others dare not trifle.

All these are examples of the lower nature taking over command.

THE HIGHER SELF. This is the true self, and one of life's most profound mysteries. Bahá'u'lláh said: *'Know, verily, that the soul is a sign of God, a heavenly gem whose reality the most learned of men hath failed to grasp, and whose mystery no mind, however acute, can hope to unravel'* (GL 158).

Life has been called man's journey in search of his own soul. Great

* This term has many definitions. Here it is used in the commonly understood sense of excessive self-concern. This should not be confused with|more|technical usage in psychology such as 'the conscious part of the personality'.

ideas of literary symbolism, like the search for the Holy Grail, relate
to this ever-present theme. When the true self is thought of in terms
of spiritual potential a magnificent and awesome picture is presented:

*O My Servants! Could ye apprehend with what wonders of My munific-
ence and bounty I have willed to entrust your souls, ye would, of a truth,
rid yourselves of attachment to all created things, and would gain a true
knowledge of your own selves – a knowledge which is the same as the
comprehension of Mine own Being.* (GL 326–7)

In addition to the explicit statement above equating true knowledge
of self with knowledge of the Manifestation, Bahá'u'lláh has stated: '*He
hath known God who hath known himself*' (GL 178). He also said: '*The
purpose of God in creating man hath been, and will ever be, to enable
him to know his Creator and to attain His Presence*' (GL 70). From these
statements many things can be inferred. Among the possibilities are the
following:

1. True knowledge of the self in a complete sense is not possible in this
lifetime.
2. Acquiring a true knowledge of the self is inseparable from gaining
knowledge of the Manifestation, hence moving toward knowing God.
3. It would, therefore, be also true that knowing more of God, through
His Manifestations, is a means by which one can acquire true knowledge of his own self.
4. A knowledge of the true self is most important. It is the purpose of
this life and a preparation for the next.

The moving toward this higher nature is the purpose of the coming
of the Manifestations. Bahá'u'lláh said:

*Through the Teachings of this Day Star of Truth every man will advance
and develop until he attaineth the station at which he can manifest all the
potential forces with which his inmost true self hath been endowed. It is
for this very purpose that in every age and dispensation the Prophets of
God and His chosen Ones have appeared amongst men . . .* (GL 68).

All the Divine Messengers brought this personal salvation, which
can be thought of as going from the lower self to the higher self.
Everyone has certain flaws in his character and tendencies toward evil
as a part of the lower nature. As one moves toward his higher nature
these less desirable characteristics become dormant. They do not
disappear, but they are no longer in command when the qualities of
character of the higher nature develop.

All religious scriptures, including the Bahá'í Writings, give generous guidance for this transformation. In one prayer the Ancient Beauty suggests man's sublime potential when He says: '*I am, O my God, but a tiny seed . . .*' Other allusions are found: '*Noble have I created thee . . .*', '*Thou art my lamp . . .*' Prayers, and works like *The Hidden Words*, reveal endless potential.

Consultation is an incredibly powerful and under-used tool for gaining knowledge of one's higher nature. It is uniquely capable of turning the spotlight of illumination on the true self through study and discussion of the Sacred Text, leading to greater understanding of the mysteries of God. This moves each one away from his lower nature and illumines the pathway to the true self.

Self-concept

The idea everyone has of himself is usually a mixture of the animal spirit and the spiritual nature with a great many other things such as fantasies, hopes, fears, loves, hates and how he sees himself in various roles. This self-concept is one of the most precious things each person has. Self-respect, courage, integrity and the sense of honour all reflect how one feels about oneself. Physical pain is hard to bear, but some find it easy compared to a torment or attack on the self-concept. Modern, sophisticated torture is often aimed as much at destroying a person's self-respect as it is at inflicting pain.

Bahá'u'lláh places backbiting, slander and gossip as among the most terrible of sins. This may be partly due to their impact on the self-concept. In the *Kitáb-i-Íqán* He said, '. . . *backbiting quencheth the light of the heart, and extinguisheth the life of the soul*' (KI 193). It is an activity that eats at the very core of a person's understanding of who he is. It affects the one spoken about, the one backbiting and the listener.

A tremendous amount of energy goes into protecting one's self-concept. People have been known to risk their lives for it. One of the causes of suicide is the despair felt when the self-concept has been destroyed – as for instance in a situation that negates a person's understanding of who he is. The threat to self-concept is thus one of the most severe threats any human being can face.

A person's self-concept may be challenged by a severe crisis such as the death of a loved one, divorce, financial loss, rejection by others, a debilitating accident, an incurable disease, a terminal illness, etc.

During the stress of one of these situations a person may become quite disoriented and act in a most peculiar manner. His self-concept has been challenged and may undergo dramatic change.

In the interest of their self-concept many people seek ways to find what they call their 'true selves'. This should not be confused with the true self mentioned earlier. It is rather an apparent self one attempts to find. Introspection and meditation are common methods for this probing; however, these devices by themselves are inadequate. There is nothing wrong with meditation or introspection; in fact, the Blessed Beauty tells us: *'Turn thy sight unto thyself that thou mayest find me standing within thee, mighty, powerful and self-subsisting'* (AHW no. 13). The problem is that unaided meditation may just as easily lead towards one's lower nature as it does to the higher one or the real true self. Reliance on the Writings, prayer and consultation are valuable companions to meditation, aiding one to receive a more balanced and better-oriented insight.

Behavior

There is frequently a difference between how a person sees himself, what he claims to believe and how he actually behaves. Specific behavior is influenced by a great many things, including the interaction of the many elements of the self.

How a person acts when he is alone or in a situation of anonymity may be different from how he behaves when in the presence of those whom he knows. His behavior when alone may be a fair gauge of how well he is doing in the struggle between his lower self and his true self. Also, we all have many roles in life and our behavior changes accordingly - we shift from one role to another depending on circumstances. When engaged in any activity what we do and how we do it is determined by who else is present and how we perceive the role that we think is expected of us. The role of a parent is different from that of the child, which in turn differs from that of a spouse. Different roles are expected in relation to adversaries or loved ones; peers or strangers; to neighbors, social, school or leisure-time acquaintances; colleagues, employers or supervisors and employees or subordinates. We feel and behave differently in each situation.

We often work hard at fulfilling our own perception of the roles we play, sometimes investing an enormous amount of energy and sense of self. This is one reason why the events mentioned earlier such as the death of a loved one or divorce or being fired or otherwise facing rejection can be so devastating: a familiar role is wiped away; it is a loss. Depending on how heavily one has invested of himself in that role, self-esteem may also suffer. A period of grieving is needed to work out the loss because, in a sense, a part of the self has vanished. Serious emotional problems can develop if one is uncomfortable with the role he is trying to fulfill.

The roles we play shape our behavior in many ways. For instance, when people become Bahá'ís they generally look upon themselves differently and change their behavior according to the new role they have adopted. For example, Bahá'u'lláh forbids the drinking of alcohol and one might reason: 'Bahá'ís do not drink. I am a Bahá'í, therefore I no longer drink.'

People can summon up enormous strength and courage to protect their self-image and the role they see themselves fulfilling. The martyrs, viewing themselves as Bahá'ís, have suffered unbelievable tortures and death rather than relinquish their Faith. A part of this is their depth of conviction reflected in their view of themselves as followers of the Blessed Beauty.

*   *   *

In consultation the mere presence of other consulting members affects each one's behavior. It is not just what is said, but the presence itself of each person that has an influence on everyone else's role. This is one of the reasons why it is best to have all nine present in a Spiritual Assembly meeting.

At its best, consultation is a mingling of true selves: a mélange of spiritual qualities. At its worst, discussion deteriorates into a collision of lower natures: a clash of egos. When deliberations are on the high level, the spiritual conference envisioned by the Master becomes a reality.

Ideally, everyone should enter consultation leaving his problems behind. However, this is not always the case — the ego is ready to leap in at any opening. For example, a basic flaw in someone's character may be that he angers easily. Through diligent efforts, concentrating on his role as a Bahá'í and focusing on Bahá'u'lláh, he may be able to overcome that flaw. However, this devil from his lower nature may only be dormant, not eliminated. If consultation deteriorates into a clash of egos, this old flaw is quickly summoned back into action and once again the soul has to struggle against this remnant of its lower nature. If consultation frequently deteriorates, there is repeated erosion of the individual's efforts to approach his higher nature. In that case the Bahá'ís have become a significant and unnecessary test for each other and one person's anger will lash out and encourage anger in others, so that contention will escalate.

This may very well be why the Center of the Covenant was so insistent that the seven requisites and two conditions be established before attempting consultation, and why the five rules of procedure are so necessary during it (see Chapter 2). These devices help each one keep proper orientation and vision. Neglect these rules and egos erupt; deterioration is guaranteed. The consulting group is then vulnerable to discussion at the lowest common denominator.

It is important to remember that the conference table represents a collection of selves and the interaction of many roles. There are ever-changing moods, personal problems and physical conditions. In fact, all the ingredients are present for incredibly complex and confusing personal interaction. Little wonder that consultation can, and does, sometimes degenerate; the wonder is that out of the labyrinth of personal foibles and idiosyncrasies a spiritual conference is possible.

It is possible only when there is constant orientation to the Covenant and reliance on the Writings and prayer. Without that orientation it is easy to slip into a quagmire of personalities and get entangled with one another's personal or personality problems.

Consultation, as a spiritual conference, really provides a triple benefit. First of all, when higher natures reign there is guaranteed illumination of the questions facing mankind. The issues of the day are examined under its brilliant searchlight. This permits the miraculous flow of heavenly bounties which produces the Kingdom of God on earth, one step at a time.

Secondly, when consulting in a spiritual conference the individual is assisted in his never-ending struggle between the higher and lower nature. This is an important factor in the life-long quest to know and worship God. Consultation helps each one find for himself the reality of his own true self.

Third, when spiritual perspectives are maintained it allows personal relationships to gravitate toward the realm of the higher nature. At the same time, this orientation prevents one from falling into the traps of the lower nature. The souls will then neither war with one another nor feed on each other's problems and inadequacies that so easily lead into the abyss of psychological confusion. The spiritual conference is the glorious melody of the diversity of humankind at its harmonious best.

Physical, Emotional and Spiritual Needs

There seems to be a great natural law that things should be kept in balance. When something is out of balance nature has a tendency to try to set it right. This is true both in physical nature and in other matters. For instance, a hungry animal searches for food. When the hunger is slight there may be little effort; when it is greater more effort will be spent; when the pangs are acute enormous effort will be expended.

This same principle works in adjusting to conditions to maintain normal, internal stability. When it gets cold blood circulation changes, animals grow heavier coats. People create a warmer environment for themselves by moving into heated houses.

People have an incredible number of needs, desires, drives and appetites in physical, emotional and spiritual matters.

Physical needs

Every human being has basic material needs which must be satisfied; they cannot be ignored. No matter what else he may accomplish he is still subject to these needs. Extensive research and much reflective thought has been devoted to understanding these needs, but it is far beyond the scope of this work to delve into these fascinating questions. In general it seems that it is the physical needs which are felt most strongly. Emotional needs, by comparison, seem more complex and subtle and often more elusive. Spiritual needs require an even higher degree of sensitivity to be noticed.

Emotional needs

Among the great number of emotional needs people have are those for love, assurance and recognition. Every experience in life affects these needs, which in turn affect future experiences. The intensity of an experience makes a great deal of difference to how one responds to each need. For example, a person who is starved of love and affection may go to great lengths to compensate for his lack of these qualities.

In general the more personally involved one is in anything the more intense will be the desire to take action. Also, the greater the intensity of a prior experience the stronger the desire to do something. For instance, a question might come up about playground safety rules. A normally responsible adult will have an interest in this, but if one has a child who is going to play there, his interest will be keener. If the adult has seen a child seriously injured on a playground, his interest is apt to be more pronounced. If one has had a child maimed or killed on play equipment, he is likely to be enormously concerned. There will also probably be a great expression of emotion.

In consultation it must be recognized that needs and emotional involvement are real. They differ from one individual to another, from time to time and from one situation to another. Effective consultation can never take place if one person belittles, minimizes or glosses over something which is of great importance to someone else. Hopes, dreams and ambitions create desires which are very important to those who have them and who will do a great deal to satisfy them. Much more will be put into a project when it becomes one's own hope and dream. Consultation allows something to become a personal goal. Then it becomes a need.

Examples abound. For instance, when a community grows to the point where a meeting-place or center is appropriate, some exciting things can happen. At first acquiring the center is a dream. Then, through consultation, the need for it is established. If it then becomes an intense desire on the part of enough members of the community and, indeed, an obsession for a few, the chances of the center becoming a reality are very much greater.

Likewise, an intense desire to see the Cause progress through more firesides, extension teaching, better children's classes, etc., is necessary for real action toward the achievement if these goals. First, the need or desire must be created. If intense enough, results will follow.

Spiritual needs

One of the subtlest yet most important needs of all has to do with the spiritual life. The Writings state that it is vital to pray daily and to read the Holy Word regularly. It is possible to go day after day and week after week ignoring this without it seeming to make much difference. When once again daily prayer and reading from the Writings are experienced refreshment appears like a soft summer breeze or gentle waves cleansing the soul. Then one is reminded how important these spiritual needs are. Sometimes it takes a severe test or crisis to force one back to the habit of daily prayer and reading. This is part of God's providence.

It is interesting to contrast spiritual needs with basic physical needs. Bahá'u'lláh ordained nineteen days during the year for His followers to refrain from food and drink from sunrise to sunset. While this discipline is difficult for some people, it can be done by practically everyone with nothing worse than some discomfort. Yet there is no time that we are told to stop praying. This suggests that daily prayer is more important to the sustaining of the spiritual life than physical food is to the physical life.

* * *

In all these areas of need – physical, emotional or spiritual – there is a comfort zone in which unfulfilled need is tolerated. This works something like a thermostat. When we get hungry enough, cold enough, angry enough, or frustrated enough we will do something to regain a balance.

No two people have the same set of needs. Nor do any two people have the same tolerance (including tolerance for consultation) with which they feel comfortable. During consultation those conferring will have different needs which must be fulfilled. Physically that may mean taking a break periodically and being attentive to special individual requirements.

The various emotional and spiritual needs which different people have are crucial to mature consultation. Sensitivity to various matters is like an antenna detecting issues which should be discussed. For example, someone may feel a need to improve the quality of children's classes because of a sense of frustration that his own child is not getting a proper Bahá'í education. That sensitivity is a gift to the entire community: the unfulfilled desire or need of that one Bahá'í may be the necessary stimulus to cause a closer look at the question.

When God has put it into someone's heart to see a problem, that person is identifying a need and has a responsibility to do something about it. He sees the need and often the best means to fulfill it. Even more important, his interest and motivation are apt to be high. There are then many ways to proceed: discussing it with others is one of the best. Through consultation the issue can be clarified because someone else is likely to see the problem differently. Thus there can be a better understanding of the issue, and a course of action (or no action) can be outlined. Consultation is the tool through which an individually perceived need can be dealt with effectively for the benefit of the entire community.

Consultation is also the best way to determine if the spiritual needs of the community are being met. Is there an effective method of deepening which attracts believers? Does prayer seem to be a natural and familiar part of the life of each Bahá'í in the community? What should be done within the community to meet the spiritual needs, expressed and unexpressed, of every heart? Is there a natural desire on the part of all to share this Message through teaching?

Perceptions

It has been said that man is the sum total of his biological nature and, in addition, everything that he has eaten, breathed, read, thought or experienced. It is agreed that past experiences together with present circumstances create the way each one views the world. This is called the 'frame of reference' which is defined as 'the set of ideas, facts, or circumstances within which something exists'. Nothing exists by itself: things have meaning only in relationship to other things, while each person's frame of reference determines how he sees things.

It is important to remember that everyone tends to think he sees things as they are. He may be tolerant of someone who sees things differently, but chances are that he really thinks the other point of view is wrong and his is right.

To illustrate this, imagine that Susan and Robert walk into a room which is painted white. Susan is wearing glasses with a yellow tint and Robert wears glasses with a red tint. Neither is aware that the glasses are tinted. Susan will see a yellow room and Robert will see a red room.

Susan may be tolerant when Robert describes the beautiful red room, although she knows Robert is wrong. The room is really yellow. Depending on her frame of reference Susan may react in any one of several different ways. She may think that Robert really said 'yellow' because that is the color she sees and what is on her mind. Therefore, when Robert says 'red' Susan may 'hear' 'yellow'. If she heard correctly, and has a kindly nature, she may think, 'Robert really meant to say "yellow" even though he said "red".' If Susan tends to confront and accuse, she is apt to think (or say): 'That Robert is color blind, playing a trick on me, stupid or lying.' Worse, if she is somewhat paranoid about Robert, she may think: 'Why does he say that? He knows the room is yellow. Is he trying to trip me up or make a fool of me? What's he up to?' An insecure Susan might think, 'There must be something wrong with me. Robert says it is red, but it looks yellow to me. I wonder why I think it's yellow. What's wrong with me?'

It would be better if Susan thought, 'Robert sees this differently from me', and let it go at that. If she wished to be assertive rather than passive or was just curious, she might think, 'Robert sees this differently. I wonder why. This difference of views could be interesting. Maybe it should be investigated.'

This simple example is not really far-fetched. It often happens in consultation that even when people have the same information their different frames of reference give various meanings to it. Background and recent experiences influence the way something is seen. A reference to authority, for instance, may induce feelings of pride and security for some while others may feel contempt and some even abject fear.

Some people are visually stimulated by information. For others the impact is aural. Still others perceive color or odor. 'The Divine Fragrances' can have specific and vivid meaning for some while seeming vague and dreamy to others. When something is being explained the frame of reference of the one speaking is reflected.

These perceptual differences among people are real, and must be taken into account in the acceptance of one another's vastly different points of view concerning the same information. It is these differing frames of reference which cause such frustration in trying to understand cultural differences. They are, for example, a major challenge in mixed marriages.

Among other things there can be a lack of understanding of why certain things are so important. What is an incidental detail for one may have enormous importance for another. Explanations as to why something is important may be unsatisfactory: even though the facts can be described, their significance may be extremely difficult to appreciate.

These differences occur in every aspect of life. Many of them are so subtle that those involved are not even aware of the source of the frustration. When different languages are used there is obvious room for misunderstanding. But beyond that lie a multitude of other variations.

Love for one's family is a strong and universal emotion. However, the role each member is expected to play within the family differs from culture to culture, and in extremely subtle ways. There are also different attitudes towards elders. Some cultures treat them with great deference and respect; their counsel is sought and cherished. In other settings their advice is often considered no longer useful.

Concepts of courtesy vary greatly. For some eye contact while talking shows sincerity, while for others it is a sign of anger or even contempt. Some groups of people are non-touchers; for others physical contact shows concern. Being the first to speak is the right of the most honored one in some cultures, while courtesy in others demands that the most honored member be the last to speak. And last but not least, one of the most elusive cultural differences is in the various senses of humor represented in the family of man. This is one of the most cherished traits, yet one of the most difficult to share.

Thinking and speaking flow in different patterns for different people. These variations in the pace or rhythm of talking complicate communication. Each may regard the other as disjointed, unclear and hard to follow. Silence is regarded by some as a necessity while others feel uncomfortable with silence and rush to fill the void with words. For some there is a need for a type of ceremonial exchange of pleasantries before important matters can be discussed. Others feel that this is a waste of time and want to get right to the issues. Once discussion has started some find it necessary to provide a long explanation of the background before making a point while others may state the point with an abruptness that the other group feels is out of context. Direct confrontation is prized by some groups as the best way to handle things while others feel it is just as important to avoid that confrontation; they may appear to talk around the point. And so it goes on.

Getting a glimpse of another culture may be like being color blind and walking into a colorful room. No matter how hard one tries, there are certain subtleties one cannot appreciate. No matter how lovingly and patiently others may try to explain the significance of color patterns, misunderstanding will always exist.

The solution is to accept and honor the value of another's frame of reference. Viewing the world differently does not mean being superior or inferior to another; it just means people see things in different ways.

The implications of all this for consultation are enormous. Everyone enters the council chamber with his own particular tinted glasses or with color blindness – his own point of view. Innumerable problems arise which must be resolved. The more different the frames of reference are, the greater the difficulties that may arise before solutions are found.

It is safe to say that every question which comes up in consultation can and will be seen from seemingly conflicting angles. Some differences are minor and do not really matter very much, but some can be extremely important. Some represent mutually exclusive views, like those of Susan and Robert: is the room red or yellow? It cannot be both. Some unresolved differences, when considered important, can generate severe hostility and antagonism.

The consultative principle given by Bahá'u'lláh can resolve these conflicts – a resolution that begins when all '*turn their faces to the Kingdom on High and ask aid from the Realm of Glory*'. Then, with attention on spiritual matters, each can be liberated from the restrictions of his own frame of reference.

A known and accepted standard, such as that established in Bahá'í Writings, can place everything in the proper perspective. When dealing with questions of taste or personal preference it is well to simply try to accept the value of the other views.

In the economic, social, cultural and political world around us these variations are handled in a different way. The tendency is to look at the differences and try to work out a compromise those involved can live with. These adjustments are often made unconsciously. In Bahá'í consultation the approach is to look away from the area of disagreement to a higher purpose. Through consultation a better perspective can be gained. Often, the nature of the difference is just not important enough to worry about.

In the setting of true consultation the impact of the different frames of reference enriches the discussion because it gives everyone a broader vision. It also helps to weave an extremely fine quality of social fabric. In other circumstances the best that could be hoped for would be a compromise of fixed opinions, leaving everyone somewhat disappointed. For Bahá'ís a richer result is produced, because the different contributions can enhance everyone's vision.

Credibility

Another kind of problem which is part of the difficulty of communication has to do with credibility, that is, the trust which one person has concerning what another says.

Differences of perception are based on the various interpretations with which information is viewed and understood. Questions of credibility challenge motivation. They erode confidence in the person himself, not just in his understanding of the situation.

It is natural to think that things really are the way one perceives them to be. If one person's view differs greatly from another's, there is a danger that a difference in perception can become a credibility problem. By way of illustration, let us review the situation with Susan (who had yellow-tinted glasses) and Robert (who had red glasses).

Susan says, 'That's a lovely yellow wall', and Robert replies, 'Yes, it is a lovely wall, only it's red.' Whereupon they smile pleasantly at each other, yet each will insist that he or she is correct. If credibility is threatened, they may each go to the wall to take a closer look. Susan will be even more convinced that the room is yellow and Robert will be even more convinced that it is red. The next step might be to take flecks of paint and examine them under a microscope. This would only reinforce their convictions. No matter how friendly and loving they may have been at the beginning, there is a good chance that by now each will start to have some doubts about the other.

The problem may not stop there. The next time Robert suggests a teaching project, Susan may very well oppose the idea as being irresponsible, while insisting there is nothing personal since she really loves Robert. The truth is, she has come to mistrust Robert's judgment and this mistrust infects all areas. Allowed to fester, the matter could erode all their confidence in each other and end up in a bitter feud. Accusations of sexism might then arise, and if they are of different races, the opportunity is ripe for racial prejudice to rear its ugly head.

The problem could be solved if Jean were to walk in with clear glasses and see that both Susan and Robert are wearing tinted glasses. Jean could point out the problem and show why they thought the way they did. Unfortunately, Jean does not always show up. And then, some Susans and Roberts may not take kindly to Jean butting in. 'She should mind her own business.' The peacemaker's role is not always well received.

How is it possible to keep a difference in perception from becoming a credibility problem? There are many ways. Here are a few suggestions:

1. Give the other person the benefit of the doubt. Not all the facts may be available. Even if they are, there may be a reasonable explanation which is not obvious. There is an old saying that love keeps you from making a judgment until an understanding is possible. Jumping to conclusions makes it much more difficult to accept a reasonable explanation.

2. Any understanding one person has is subject to error. It may come close to truth, but absolute, complete understanding is rare. Each one may be right from his own point of view.

3. The different perception which someone else has may be a point of view which is important, in order to get a more complete understanding of the situation.

4. Never be afraid to be wrong. When proven wrong the only thing which can be hurt is the ego; and this can be beneficial spiritually.

5. Remember that all Bahá'ís are really working for the same goals. All are under the shadow of the Covenant and share in a love for that Covenant. The fundamental desire of every sincere believer is whatever serves the best interests of the Cause.

6. Put the differences themselves in proper perspective. Do the varying opinions really matter? Is it important to the Cause of God to find the truth about the matter in dispute? If not, let each live with his own understanding. It is more important to be united than to be right. Let Susan enjoy her yellow wall and let Robert be happy with his red one.

7. Differences in perception simply reflect a part of the wide range of diversity in the human family.

Differences of perspective do exist. They are a part of the charm, the diversity, the splendor of the family of man; they are also necessary for effective consultation. It is from these variations that opinions are able to clash, to create that spark of truth. When the differences become credibility problems the nature of consultation changes. Emotions take over. The clean, sharp clash of opinions which produced the sparks of truth are lost. Rather than ideas clashing, personalities and egos begin to collide. Then only heat, rather than light, is produced and consultation degenerates into an encounter of egos. For this reason every effort should be exerted to keep differences in perception from becoming problems of credibility.

NINE

The Search for Truth

Understanding, Real and Imagined

Bahá'u'lláh praises highly the gift of understanding. He says:

Know thou that, according to what thy Lord, the Lord of all men, hath decreed in His Book, the favors vouchsafed by Him unto mankind have been, and will ever remain, limitless in their range. First and foremost among these favors, which the Almighty hath conferred upon man, is the gift of understanding. His purpose in conferring such a gift is none other except to enable His creatures to know and recognize the one true God – exalted be His glory. This gift giveth man the power to discern the truth in all things, leadeth him to that which is right, and helpeth him to discover the secrets of creation. (GL 194)

He goes on to talk about '*the power of vision*' as being lower in rank and then He speaks of the other senses.

The fact that the Ancient Beauty gives understanding such a high station suggests several things. First of all, anything which can give '*the power to discern the truth in all things*' leads '*to that which is right*' and helps discover '*the |secrets| of |creation*' must be extremely profound. It must involve much more than knowledge or the accumulation of information. According to the dictionary, to understand is to have a 'clear or complete idea' and be 'thoroughly familiar with the character and propensities'. It also means to 'grasp the meaning' as well as 'the nature, significance or explanation of something'. A 'sympathetic or tolerant attitude' is also among the meanings. This '*first and foremost . . . favor*', this '*gift of understanding*' also involves combining and organizing knowledge, assigning levels of importance to various facts, knowing the implications of information and being aware of how different details affect one another.

True understanding

True understanding, in a complete sense, may not be as common as is often thought. Indeed, it is likely that no mere mortal can ever have an absolute understanding of anything. Everyone is limited by the information available and by his previous training, experience, cultural or social background, physical well-being, degree of interest and individual capacities and perceptions. The Blessed Báb made reference to this basic limitation when he said: '. . . *no mind or vision, however keen or discriminating, can ever grasp the nature of the most insignificant of Thy signs*' (USBP 126).

Instead, there are many different kinds of understanding and each of them has various degrees of completeness. What one feels he 'knows' may be correct, but only in terms of a particular level of partial comprehension; it may or may not be adequate for a larger purpose. The important thing is whether or not the understanding which a person has is adequate for the needs which must be served. For example, a child, an average adult, an electrician and an electrical engineer are all apt to have different understandings of electricity – how it works and how it can be used. One may have a complex comprehension which includes a great deal of theoretical understanding. Another may have a practical and serviceable skill while still another may have quite a superficial concept. The child might have no real concept of electricity. In spite of these differences each has certain areas of competence and for each there would be many things beyond his understanding.

It is fortunate that complete comprehension is not necessary. In the above examples all four can make quite good use of the limited knowledge they have. The child may know that by turning on a switch a light goes on. He really does not need to have any more profound insight than that in order to get by quite well as a child. Danger lies in trying to work beyond one's competence. If the light switch does not work, the child could hurt himself if he tried to take it apart to fix it; that is beyond his level of understanding.

Feeling of understanding

Most people need to feel they understand what is going on. One often experiences frustration, uneasiness, increased agitation and stress when one does not comprehend something. For example, a loud noise and the shaking of a house can be quite disturbing if one does not know what has happened. A rush to the window may show that a large truck nearby has just dumped a load of gravel on the ground. Once one understands, it is possible to relax and go back to other concerns.

People have a wide range of tolerance for things they do not understand. Some people make snap judgments or jump to conclusions. Others are content to wait patiently until matters become clear.

The 'feeling' of understanding may or may not be indicative of any real understanding, but the need for that feeling is great. In part this is because it is so closely related to the other needs people have. Three of these – a sense of control, a feeling of being heard and a feeling of receiving an explanation – are extremely important to consultation.

Control

When one feels he knows what is going on, he knows how to react and can feel in control of himself in the given situation. A feeling of understanding is necessary to that sense of control. This in turn affects a person's feeling of well-being. In general the less sure one is of oneself the greater one's need to figure things out quickly and regain some semblance of control. This is what causes people to jump to conclusions. A feeling of understanding is then achieved, although it may be inaccurate, hasty or incomplete. This common tendency complicates consultation.

Being heard

A sense of communication is very much part of understanding and acceptance. In consultation people can more easily accept a decision which is not in their favor if they feel they have been listened to. If people are not given a chance to be heard, they may never understand why a certain decision was reached. This can build resentment. The need to be heard is often more important than the information which is being conveyed. It cannot be neglected without inviting problems.

Explanation

Closely related to the above is the feeling of getting an explanation.

People can accept a decision much more readily when they are given a reason. It is technically correct that a Spiritual Assembly does not have to answer to the members of the community, but it is wise to share as much as possible. Otherwise a sense of aloofness or even arrogance may develop. A pattern of receiving explanations for actions builds confidence and makes it easier to accept something when no explanation is possible. 'I know they must have a good reason' is likely to be the conclusion. When there is a pattern of withholding information the result eventually will become, 'Now what are they up to?'

What is it that makes a person feel that he understands something? The feeling itself develops in several ways. Among them is the feeling of being comfortable with that which is known. When all the information seems to fit together in such a way as to make sense, that is the sensation felt.

It is really this feeling of understanding which provides many direct blessings. This is the gift that more than anything else permits one of the greatest sensations – the thrill of discovery. Some level of understanding must be present in order to appreciate the wonders of nature, science, music, art, other cultures, humor, literature and so on. This is the feeling that can soothe frayed nerves, give relief and contribute to the healing of a wound. It enables one to deal with an issue, put it aside and never be troubled by it again. Or a solution to a difficult problem often becomes obvious once one feels he understands the situation. Determination and the means of taking appropriate action generally accompany that sensation of understanding. Renewed confidence, a sense of direction, and the feeling of being in control are among the results.

Even a problem with no good solution can be accepted when there is a sense of purpose, a knowledge of how it fits into the larger picture or just plain resignation. All these come from the feeling of understanding, as do the renewed sense of well-being, the confidence that everything can be all right and the assurance that life will go on.

We are constantly being exposed to new information and continually need to fit the new into the pattern with what is already understood. The mind ever seeks either to combine the new with what it knows already or to find a means to reject the new information.

What actually happens is that in order to make sense out of new information the mind does many creative things. If the facts do not fit together, the imagination works overtime until some explanation emerges. It is like having a jigsaw puzzle with some pieces missing. The mind creates and supplies the missing pieces and may even change some existing pieces in order to make them all fit. At best, the results come close to the true situation. At worst, there may be a great distortion: the conclusion can be quite different from the truth – even the opposite. However, the person may feel he knows and understands because the pieces fit in his mind regardless of whether the result is right or wrong.

Understanding develops in many different ways. Sometimes things just seem to slip together and there is no conscious awareness of knowing to contrast with not knowing. At other times all the facts may be present but they just do not fit into a meaningful pattern. All of a sudden there may be a flash of insight and the picture jells. From then on the conclusion seems self-evident – it may be hard to remember why one did not understand before, or even that there was a problem in the first place.

Once a feeling of understanding is set, it is sometimes very difficult to dislodge or change. This is especially true when the facts are correct. Two people may have the same facts but because of their differences they will see things differently. If one person has a trusting nature his imagination may make the pieces fit together with a message that everything is all right. If another person has a suspicious nature the inventions of his mind make the same facts fit together with the message that something is wrong. Each may be convinced that he 'knows'.

Illusion of knowing

People have a tendency to see things the way they wish them to be. Information is generally interpreted to support a strongly held, preconceived notion. A conviction, no matter how strongly held, can only come close to the true situation, even at best. The problem is that many counterfeits of true understanding exist and create enormous difficulties because they give the illusion of knowing. The most common is misunderstanding, in which one or more elements are wrong, missing or viewed improperly. These mistakes may be quite innocent, yet can cause great difficulty.

Another more serious counterfeit of real understanding is the distorted view. Here there may even be an element of malice involved sometimes. In that case the one holding the distorted view may have little interest in correcting it. In any event, disentangling distorted and twisted understandings is extremely difficult.

One of the worst counterfeits comes from pure invention or fabrication. A person imagines something to be so. If convinced that the story is true, it is extremely difficult for him to change his conviction. It is based on conjecture in which an explanation is created to account for something that is unknown. A classic example was the idea that the sun moved so that it 'rose' and 'set' over a flat and motionless earth. This conjecture was believed for centuries to be true; it was held to be a 'known fact' and was most difficult to put aside. Some people suffered greatly because of this mistaken understanding. The incorrect descriptions of a 'rising' or 'setting' sun have remained a permanent part of the language.

Ironically, the sensation of knowing is genuine and can be just as exhilarating whether the understanding is true, partial or one of the counterfeits. Often there is great eagerness to accept *any* explanation of something, just to discover a 'reason' and have something to cling to. 'That's it! That's it!' one may exclaim with great vigor. Holding firmly to a feeling of knowing feels good and provides a sense of security. Many strongly-held convictions develop because of the *feeling* of understanding with no real substance for support. Much religious bigotry and fanaticism is the result of this process.

Another trouble with counterfeits is that they are usually woven in with correct but partial understandings. Extracting the truth from the web of the false is no easy task.

The strength of someone's conviction is another matter which varies greatly, and can range all the way from indifferent uncertainty to a firm feeling that one *knows* what is true. One can feel just as confident whether right or wrong. It has nothing to do with sincerity – one may have the purest of motives and be sincerely wrong. Strength of conviction does not ensure truth; it only makes correcting an error more difficult.

These counterfeits of true understanding are sometimes extremely difficult to detect. Sometimes one's sincerity itself makes the counterfeit seem real. One way to tell the difference is by results. Does the understanding produce an attitude of judging or forbearance? Does it create healing or contention? Does it attract or repel others? Another standard is one's willingness to explore other ideas. Reluctance to look at other views suggests that one is holding a counterfeit understanding that cannot withstand the test of close examination.

Understanding from Consultation

It may be seen that true understanding is really quite rare. When those consulting come together, each is equipped with his own partial understanding. Through consultation they share what each has to offer. The better elements from each serve to enrich, complete and improve everyone else's comprehension. In another setting these different views might be competitive. In consultation they are complementary.

Information is often missing; consultation supplies missing pieces. Twisted or distorted understandings may regain their proper shape when stretched, pushed and pulled by the differing views set forth. The distinction between a true or a counterfeit understanding can be made abundantly clear under the searchlight of illumined consultation.

When the counterfeit is conjecture consultation shines at its best. A complete change is possible as the false is discovered, dispelled, put aside and the gem of a luminous new truth stands in its place. This is what the Beloved was describing when He said, '*Consultation bestoweth greater awareness and transmuteth conjecture into certitude*' (CC no. 3).

Any understanding resulting from consultation is much more likely to be free from error than that which a person reasons out for himself. Infallibility, however, is reserved to the Universal House of Justice.

Not only has consultation been given a unique station as the '*bestower*' of understanding, but understanding is necessary for effective consultation. At first glance that may look like circular reasoning. It is not; rather there is an interdependence and mutual benefit which contributes to both processes.

The first step in decision-making using consultation is to understand the problem or the background situation. (See Chapter 3.) Only when that has been accomplished can consultation provide proper solutions. The final result is progress and improved total understanding.

There is still one major obstacle which stands in the way of attaining higher levels of understanding through consultation. That is when one or more of those consulting persist in holding on to preconceived notions or jealously guard their own special interests. This problem can be devastating; it betrays inflexibility and unwillingness to change. Strongly-held points of view actually help to produce the clash of ideas which are needed for the sparks of truth to fly. Inflexible convictions, on the other hand, interfere with effective consultation.

When a person thinks he 'knows' what is true, consultation can actually threaten his sense of control. It takes great maturity, self-discipline and self-confidence for anyone to suspend his own strongly-held convictions or special interests to allow consultation an unfettered chance to develop.

Some people find changing their opinions easy; others find it extremely difficult. The greater the intensity of the consultation, the more emotionally involved one is with the subject, and the more convinced one is that he is correct, the harder it is to change.

Giving up personal opinions may be a psychological experience like going through the sound barrier. Nonetheless it is necessary to break through that barrier in order to find the truth. The understanding achieved may be a hard-won and valued prize. It should come as no surprise that this *'first and foremost. . . favor'*, this *'gift'*, takes great effort to achieve. Nor should it be a surprise that, even at best, each person's view of anything is limited and liable to error no matter how solid and secure that opinion may be.

About the gift of understanding several features stand out:
1. The importance given this wondrous experience as the first and foremost of the favors is, by itself, worthy of reflection.
2. There are many benefits from understanding, as suggested earlier. However, it has but one *purpose.* That is '*to enable His creatures to know and recognize the one true God'.* All else is secondary. Understandings which do not contribute to that purpose are really divine forces gone astray.
3. Consultation as the '*bestower of understanding*' plays an extremely significant role in the Divine Purpose mentioned above.

4. The fact that consultation is an active process suggests that knowing and recognizing God are neither passive nor things that can be finally accomplished. They are, instead, acquired by degrees according to capacity, which then expands with the very activities that contribute to greater understanding.

5. There is nothing more private and personal than one's opinion and point of view. However, consultation establishes a valuable link between the collective world and the most intimate and secret thoughts. One's private world of understanding is enriched and expanded during the collective activity of consultation.

6. The world about us is confusing, contradictory, inconsistent and capricious. *It is imperfect, yet filled with perfections.* It is difficult, yet brimming with wonder; a never-ending source of awe. Each one's view is limited, narrow and distorted, leading more to speculation than to knowledge. Yet through the marvel of consultation nurturing the gift of understanding, individual vision is expanded, horizons are pushed back, distortions are reshaped to more appropriate forms and guesswork is replaced by knowledge.

7. Every time there is true consultation in assemblies, committees, groups, among friends or colleagues, in families and social activities greater understanding enters the human fold. With this understanding benefits and favors come pouring forth from on High. All the while there is fulfillment of God's one desire and purpose: *'to enable His creatures to know and recognize the one true God'.*

Four Methods of Comprehension

'There are four criteria or standards of judgment by which the human mind reaches its conclusions' (PUP 253), 'Abdu'l-Bahá tells us, and elsewhere he says, *'there are only four accepted methods of comprehension — that is to say, the realities of things are understood by these four methods'* (SAQ 297). He describes these as

1. sense perception
2. reason
3. tradition
4. inspiration

The implications of this for consultation are fascinating to think about. We may observe that most people tend to prefer one of these methods to the others. This is not something one can be rigid about –

we all accept sense perceptions, use reason, have some traditional background and are subject to degrees of inspiration. These methods do not represent personality types: many people may use different methods at different times or even simultaneously. Yet there is a tendency for one method of comprehension to be the most typical and comfortable for each person.

Two people relying on different methods may reach different conclusions with the same information, and an appreciation of these different methods is thus vital in consultation, helping the individual to validate the contributions made by others.

These four methods of comprehension have several things in common:

1. A person can get through life reasonably well using any one of the four.

2. No one of them is any better or any worse than any other.

3. People often cannot understand someone whose method tends to be different from their own. Sometimes suspicion or distrust is aroused because of this.

4. Enormous confusion can result in consultation because of these different methods of comprehension. People are said to 'be on different wave lengths', or talking 'right past' each other.

5. The variety can either become a source of richness in consultation or create unbelievable chaos, depending on the degree to which these differences are accepted.

People who rely on one particular method tend to gravitate toward others whose method is similar to their own. The Bahá'í Faith is meant for all mankind, which includes people using each method of comprehension. This brings a built-in conflict to the community of the Greatest Name which would be impossible to resolve without the blessing of consultation. Each system makes a special contribution to consultation and each creates a special challenge.

Sense Perception

Anyone who relies primarily on sense perception as a standard for truth is inclined to see things 'as they are'. 'What are the facts?' may well be the first question asked in discussing any subject. An advantage of this type of thinking in consultation is insistence on getting the facts, acting on what is known and caution about conjecture or assumptions. A disadvantage is that action may not be as important as analysis and reducing things to a cogent summary statement can become an end in and of itself. There may also be a reluctance to stray very far from that which can be clearly demonstrated and proven. This may seem cumbersome, tedious or inhibiting to others.

Reason

The one who relies on reason or cognitive processes, 'thinks things through'. He is apt to be rational and logical. He may well explore new ideas which are logical extensions beyond that which is known. This may lead either to abstract knowledge or into the uncharted seas of new ventures. In consultation this thinking has the value of showing a logical connection between various matters and the facts at hand. It can also provide a view which may go beyond those immediate facts. Problems, however, can develop if others see it as 'getting out on a limb'. They may find it hard to follow reasoning which goes very far beyond what can be readily seen. They then become disenchanted, impatient or suspicious of seemingly obscure conclusions.

Tradition

The individual who relies on tradition, precedent or past experiences for his standard of what is right may desire order and clear-cut procedures. Structure and consistency might be the highly regarded standard. In consultation this valuable contribution leads to organization, following procedures and clear-cut guidelines. Problems can arise when administrative procedures are applied too rigidly, for this can unintentionally squash enthusiasm and stifle creativity. Creative, energetic Bahá'ís, rather than being inspired to work harder for the Cause, can become discouraged and driven away from Bahá'í activity when there is a feeling of rigidity or when there is too much structure or too many detailed instructions.

Inspiration

This is truly one of the most fascinating and multi-faceted of the four criteria or methods of approaching truth. People from all walks of life have experienced inspiration varying from the simple to the profound. Through this precious bounty, gifts of great value have been realized which have proved beneficial to all mankind.

Some people rarely, if ever, experience what can be called inspiration. Many others, regardless of their customary method of thinking, have enjoyed its enrichment. There are still others for whom inspiration or feeling or intuition has become the dominant influence and source of guidance for their lives.

Inspiration is a source of guidance, but it is also full of potential hazards. The Master affirmed that inspiration '*is the influx of the human heart*'. He also warned that '*satanic promptings which afflict mankind . . . are the influx of the heart also. How shall we differentiate between them?*' (PUP 22). Great difficulties can arise because what someone may think of as '*inspiration*' turns out instead to be '*satanic promptings*'.

The Guardian was even more explicit about the dangers of relying only on one's own inner promptings. From a letter written on his behalf we read, 'With regard to your question as to the value of intuition as a source of guidance for the individual; implicit faith in our intuitive powers is unwise, but through daily prayer and sustained effort one can discover, though not always and fully, God's Will intuitively. Under no circumstances, however, can a person be absolutely certain that he is recognizing God's Will, through the exercise of his intuition. It often happens that the latter results in completely misrepresenting the truth and thus becomes a source of error rather than of guidance' (LG 577).

By itself, inspiration or intuition can lead to clarity or fuzzy thinking; to lofty thoughts or depraved ones; to the brilliant or the irrational. However, inspiration serves an extremely important role in consultation. Those who rely heavily on intuition as the guidance for their lives offer a source of ideas and sensitivity not common to others. The flash of insight experienced by those consulting often produces vigorous and exciting material for the conference table. Ideas developed during consultation itself are often a form of inspiration.

Illuminating the Search

Everyone becomes used to and comfortable with his accustomed '*method of comprehension*'. Other '*avenues of knowledge*', being unfamiliar, may seem strange and the valuable contributions others have to offer may not be understood and appreciated as easily as one's own accustomed way.

For example, someone who is attached to just one approach may think: 'All our problems could be managed easily if people would just stick to the facts.' Someone else is apt to think: 'All would go well if people would only do what is reasonable.' Yet another may think: 'If we would only follow established procedures these matters could be taken care of quite easily.' Still another may think: 'If we were more "spiritual" we would be inspired to do the right thing.' None of these approaches is wrong. They are simply different and each one reflects a particular approach to evaluating information and problem-solving. The fact remains, however, that these very differences can lead to faulty and confusing communication. Something which may seem obvious to one person is quite unclear to another. In listening to something which seems perfectly clear to the person talking, someone else may think: 'What in the world is he talking about?' This can happen simply because the method of comprehension of the one talking is different from the methods of those listening.

Each method by itself has value, but is imperfect and susceptible to error. Commenting on these standards 'Abdu'l-Bahá said that something which can withstand the rigors of all four can be relied on as correct (PUP 255). In consultation, using all four approaches mentioned above would certainly produce good results. The Master gave some highly illuminating advice when He said:

these four are . . . avenues of knowledge, and all of them are faulty and unreliable. What then remains? How shall we attain the reality of knowledge? By the breaths and promptings of the Holy Spirit, which is light and knowledge itself. Through it the human mind is quickened and fortified into true conclusions and perfect knowledge. (PUP 22)

Generally, everyone would agree that it is desirable to find '*the reality of knowledge*', as suggested by 'Abdu'l-Bahá. It may be difficult, however, to agree exactly what '*the breaths and promptings of the Holy Spirit*' really are.

Consultation uniquely solves the question of how to discover those promised '*promptings*'. The Master said, '*If a few souls gather in a beloved meeting with the feelings of the Kingdom . . . The Holy Spirit will strengthen them and the hosts of the Supreme Concourse will render them victorious*' (CC 11). That is, through consultation the '*promptings of the Holy Spirit*' enable '*true conclusions*' to emerge from the varied assessments present. The different methods of thinking or different standards or criteria of truth complement one another through their compensating strengths. This reduces the chances of serious mistakes and increases the chances of good decisions. That way the Holy Spirit distills truth from the different processes and standards, leaving the inherent weakness of each behind.

It is the power of the Covenant, surrounding the marvel of consultation, which makes it possible for differing approaches to enrich the
endeavors of man. The presence of the different approaches keeps
consultation from getting unbalanced. The love of Bahá'u'lláh prevents
these differences from becoming a source of contention as they become
harmonized, leading the consulting body ever closer to the elusive
truth.

Unity in Diversity

On March 19, 1973, the Universal House of Justice wrote a letter in
which they said in part, 'It should be borne in mind that all consultation is aimed at arriving at a solution to a problem . . .' (CC no. 47).

There would be little argument that Bahá'ís are interested in truth.
There may, however, be tremendous differences of understanding of
what truth is. Bahá'u'lláh has said: *'No two men can be found who
may be said to be outwardly and inwardly united'* (GL 218). It is
because of this very lack of unity that consultation is necessary. Both
Bahá'u'lláh and the Center of the Covenant have often mentioned
consultation in terms of illumination and the finding of the truth.
Looking upon each perspective as a light, the idea is to place as much
illumination as possible on the question being discussed. A spiritual
attitude is the means of focusing light on the question. If all points of
view are pretty much alike, the light will be intensified but come from
the same general area. This can also cause deeper shadows on another
aspect of the question. If the points of view or the lights come from
widely separated points, illumination shines on all sides of the
question.

Without a spiritual basis for the consultation, the lights from each
point of view will not be properly focused. Instead of pointing at the
question they will wander. This will result in lights pointing at each
other and blinding one another rather than being used for illumination. Rather than the issue becoming more clear, shadows will reflect
from the poorly-used lights. The result will be that the issue itself will
receive little illumination, contention will develop and the truth will
remain hidden.

For example, let us assume a Local Spiritual Assembly wishes to
discuss race unity and how to cleanse the community of the taint of

prejudice. There will be some serious limitations if the only ones consulting on this important question are all black, or all American Indians, or all Caucasians or all Iranians or all Asians or all anything else. Their experiences and perspectives are less likely to contribute to as complete an understanding as would be possible if differing views were represented.

If the group were made up of people from different backgrounds and discussed the same question, the results would probably be different. First of all there is much more danger. With greater divergence the chances of misunderstanding increase. Also, people are then opening themselves to possible hurt. They become more vulnerable to a clash of egos.

To avoid these dangers a spiritual climate is crucial. Then, by the power of the Covenant, discussion is elevated from the clash of egos to an exchange of the higher natures. Under a spiritual discipline a more complete, well-rounded illumination of the question is possible. Each person's contribution is then like a light aimed on the question from a different angle. Then, under the illumination of consultation, improved understanding emerges, the truth is found and the best course of action can be worked out.

There may still be a question of how to use that newly-found truth. The truth of any situation is a tool which can be used either beneficially or harmfully. Truth can be used as a shovel to scrape away the debris of misconceptions, ignorance, or prejudice. Truth can also be used as a club with which to hit someone over the head.

'*The Great Being saith: The heaven of divine wisdom is illumined with the two luminaries of consultation and compassion*'(TB 168). Once truth is found through consultation that is only half of the task. In order to complete the illumination compassion needs to be added. Taken together, consultation and compassion provide illumination of any question, involving the mind, the heart and the soul in a brilliant enlightenment.

In spiritual conference, then, when there are similar points of view light is intensified, but some areas may be missed. The greater the difference, the more the whole question can be flooded with light, as long as each one keeps in mind his relationship with the Covenant, focuses on the question and maintains a compassionate perspective. The result will be a broader-based decision, resting on mature understanding, born of different points of view. This is illumined consultation; a truly spiritual conference.

TEN

Spiritual Battles

Whatever else may be said of this life, it is brimming with tests, trials and tribulations. They come as an integral part of everyday life. Even routine daily activities serve as a continual testing or proving ground.

Tests and Difficulties

The highest level of suffering was experienced by the Manifestation Himself. The price Bahá'u'lláh paid to bring the Revelation of God to man was enormous. The Wronged One said:

The Ancient Beauty hath consented to be bound with chains that mankind may be released from its bondage, and hath accepted to be made a prisoner within this most mighty Stronghold that the whole world may attain unto true liberty. He hath drained to its dregs the cup of sorrow, that all the peoples of the earth may attain unto abiding joy, and be filled with gladness. (GL 99)

This passage is a clear demonstration of the highest and noblest use of tests and suffering. The value of every other kind of problem may be measured against its standard. The Blessed Beauty shared His agonies with us to help us keep perspective. '*We disclosed to thee a glimmer of the woes that have come upon Us, that thou mayest be made aware of Our suffering and patiently endure thy sorrows*' (GL 296).

Referring to the sufferings endured in the path of God by any who would follow the divine path He said, '*Know ye that trials and tribulations have, from time immemorial, been the lot of the chosen Ones of God and His beloved, and such of His servants as are detached from all else but Him . . .*'(GL 129).

The Báb was even more specific. In a prayer, He revealed the following: '*Thou wilt never cause tribulations to befall any soul unless Thou desirest to exalt his station in Thy celestial Paradise and to buttress his heart in this earthly life*' (SWB 215).

There is no growth without pain. Entrance into this world has its 'birth pangs'. Pain seems a part of every stage of life. Even the process of teething is a difficult period. In the Bahá'í community one result of new expansion is the guarantee of additional tests. All this involves suffering.

The Master tells us that there are two kinds of tests. '*One kind is to test the soul, and the other is punishment for actions*' (DAL 89, no. 1). Of the first kind He said: '*Tests are benefits from God, for which we should thank Him. Grief and sorrow do not come to us by chance, they are sent to us by the Divine mercy for our own perfecting*' (DAL 89, no. 2). In another place He said: '*Just as the plow furrows the earth deeply, purifying it of weeds and thistles, so suffering and tribulation free man from the petty affairs of this worldly life until he arrives at a state of complete detachment*' (DAL 90, no. 3).

As these tests appear they bring some marvelous, if unwelcome, opportunities for detachment. It is far beyond the scope of this book to consider the vast range of benefits available from tests and difficulties. But here are just a few ideas from the limitless mine of possibilities.

> Priorities can be suddenly re-evaluated. A crisis has a way of clearing the head of trivia. Old truths are validated.

> Tests provide a good time for self-appraisal. A good measure of a person (or a consulting group) is shown by the types of things which are upsetting or which slip by unnoticed. For example, if an assembly is disturbed by a poorly-prepared committee report but is indifferent as to whether or not there is teaching, love and unity in the community, it may be in the process of failing a test.

> It is a time for trying new things as old reliable doors close and the untried must be attempted.

> Tests are reminders of one's limitations and mortality. They redefine the sense of self.

> Nothing can bond hearts together like sharing mutual hardships.

They also link us to the bounties of God and prepare us for advanced forms of service. Speaking of various types of tests through persecutions the Master said: ' *Unless a servant in the Cause of God is subjected to all these persecutions he is not fitted to spread the Heavenly Message of Glad Tidings. Follow 'Abdu'l-Bahá! Let nothing hinder or defeat you. God is your helper and God is invincible*' (sw iv, no. 5, p. 89).

Sources of Tests

Not all people undergo the same tests: what is a problem for one person may make no difference at all to someone else. They come in the individual's areas of weakness. 'Abdu'l-Bahá said:

Tests are a means by which a soul is measured as to its fitness, and proven out by its own acts. God knows its fitness beforehand, and also its unpreparedness, but man, with an ego, would not believe himself unfit unless proof were given him. Consequently his susceptibility to evil is proven to him when he falls into the tests, and the tests are continued until the soul realizes its own unfitness, then remorse and regret tend to root out the weakness.

The same test comes again in greater degree, until it is shown that a former weakness has become a strength, and the power to overcome evil has been established. (sw vi, no. 6, p. 45)

From this it follows that tests which occur in the area where someone is strong may not even be recognized as tests. A person's culture, age, experience, life-style all play a part in whether or not a particular test will be handled well or will present a serious problem.

While Bahá'ís in some parts of the world are attaining the crown of martyrdom, others face different problems. The Guardian warned, '. . . how often we seem to forget the clear and repeated warnings of our beloved Master, who, in particular during the concluding years of His mission on earth, laid stress on the "*severe mental tests*" that would inevitably sweep over His loved ones of the West – tests that would purge, purify and prepare them for their noble mission in life' (BA 50).

From outside the Faith enemies do what they can to harm the Bahá'ís, including martyring their leaders. This happens when there is inadequate official protection for the innocent. In other places some

Bahá'ís are caught by the increasing pressure of the decadent society around them. Instead of falling victim to bloodthirsty and fanatical elements, they are sucked into the vortex of greed, vices of the flesh and other influences of a world which glorifies self-serving, pleasure-oriented and superficial values. Less obvious, but just as harmful, are the pressures for achievement, success or just survival in an increasingly materialistic world. From inside the Faith, too, it may be a severe test to work with those whose cultural habits, priorities and mannerisms are far different from one's own. The institutions themselves may make requests which become severe tests. All this may be inferred from the *Tablet of Aḥmad* in which there is a plea for steadfastness even if '. . . *all the heavens and the earth arise against thee*' (USBP 211).

The emotional, physical and nervous energy required to cope with the growing frustrations of Western civilization steadily erodes the desire for spiritual things. Some people become too tired or apathetic to serve their Faith. While subtle, this is a pernicious attack on the community of the Greatest Name. It is hard to fight because it is an attack without a clearly defined attacker. It is truly a '*severe mental test*'.

Attacks from outside the Faith – some brutal and vicious, others delicate and subtle – as well as problems from within – from weakness in the Covenant, weakness of character or personality conflicts – are bound to increase as the vitality and prestige of the Cause expands during its relentless, God-impelled rendezvous with destiny.

Stress

All life involves stress – in fact, the opposite of stress is death. Stress is really a preparation for action. It is a tension, like a rubber band being stretched, so that some action can be produced.

Mild stress is not only beneficial, it is essential. This is true both for individuals and consulting groups. When stress becomes excessive or is denied a normal condition within which to respond it becomes distress and that produces problems. But with mild stress there is an increase in available energy, sharpened senses and greater alertness. When stress increases to a point of urgency there is still a beneficial aspect. It increases creativity and innovation. Thinking becomes keener and more penetrating. Stress has also been known to heal. All kinds of cures, from hiccups to paralysis to amnesia, have been credited to stress. People have conquered great obstacles because they were either motivated or made angry enough to overcome complacency. Personality conflicts have been known to evaporate when people are bonded through a common crisis.

On the other hand, impulsive, erratic, frantic, irrational and bizarre behavior and panic can come from stress when it is too intense or prolonged. This is distress. The mind can be flooded with a rush of incomplete and contradictory thoughts. Reasoning processes can become clouded and judgment impaired. Confidence in one's abilities and accomplishments can be eroded. There can be prolonged strange behavior.

The reaction to stress varies greatly from one person to another and from one situation to another. The results are not always predictable. Indeed, stress produced from a crisis situation may immobilize some people, rendering them incapable of taking appropriate action or seeking a reasonable course of action.

Some people, on the other hand, become as if catapulted to new and hitherto unknown heights, demonstrating great qualities of crisis management and leadership. They find a more acute clarity of vision and seem to respond automatically in an appropriate manner. Occasionally, when the crisis is over, such people have been themselves amazed at how well they dealt with the situation.

As the pressures of the modern world become more intense a growing latent power develops. If not directed properly, this energy becomes a destructive force. Through the teachings and the marvel of consultation the power born of stress can be harnessed and used beneficially.

This happens when people have been accustomed to consulting on ordinary matters. Then, even under pressure, it is natural to consult. The discussion assumes greater intensity because of the stress. Those consulting get to the heart of the matter quickly and find a course of action with the fewest false starts. The chance of being diverted from the main aspect of the problem is also reduced. The net result is that the greater energy and vision which come from a high sense of urgency can be utilized. At the same time irrational activity and frantic diversions are avoided and tendencies toward panic are dissipated, all because of seasoned consultation.

Tests, difficulties and stress there will be. Dealing with them effectively is the challenge. Furthermore, as long as there are people, problems are a certainty. Nowhere in Bahá'í literature is it suggested that a time will ever come when there will be no more tests; on the contrary, the Writings refer to tests and difficulties as a necessary part of growth. They are a part of life itself, affecting the individual, his close associates and his entire community.

Searching for Solutions

Since there is no escape from problems it is fortunate that special methods of dealing with tribulations have been given to man. In this day, through consultation, the range of possibilities for dealing with tests has increased vastly.

When a believer has a problem concerning which he must make a decision he has several courses open to him. If it is a matter that affects the interests of the Faith he should consult with the appropriate Assembly or committee, but individuals have many problems which are purely personal and there is no obligation upon them to take such problems to the institutions of the Faith; indeed, when the needs of the teaching work are of such urgency it is better if the friends will not burden their Assemblies with personal problems that they can solve by themselves.
   A Bahá'í who has a problem may wish to make his own decision upon it after prayer and after weighing all the aspects of it in his own mind; he may prefer to seek the counsel of individual friends or of professional counselors such as his doctor or lawyer so that he can consider such advice when making his decision; or in a case where several people are involved, such as a family situation, he may want to gather together those who are affected so that they may arrive at a collective decision. There is also no objection whatever to a Bahá'í asking a group of people to consult together on a problem facing him. (CC no. 47)

   No matter how a problem was caused, it is possible either to benefit from it or to suffer more than is necessary. Even problems caused by poor judgment or wrongdoing have the potential for good results.

Facing the problem
Any issue which is important enough to be a problem must be resolved in some way. Sometimes it is a temporary condition and time takes care of it. Other problems seem to disappear when placed in a better perspective. However, suppressing a problem or keeping

something bottled inside oneself can make the results worse than the original issue. An unresolved problem will express itself at some time in some way and generally results in a more serious problem. Dealing with a persistent and troubling issue is imperative; the sooner it is done the easier it will be.

This principle also applies to consulting groups. Ignoring a problem in the community because it is unpleasant often makes the ultimate problem worse. Difficult though it may be, facing it directly and early is generally best. As with individuals, resolving the problem may take time and have to go through many separate steps.

The cleansing

A simple formula has been given by Bahá'u'lláh through which both individuals and consulting groups may derive benefit from any problem: 'Remembrance of Me cleanseth all things from defilement, could ye but perceive it' (GL 294–5). This is a marvelous promise. 'All things' means 'all things'! It is a cleansing which draws the sparkling truth of divine virtue from even the most difficult problem. There is no test, no problem, no hell which is so bad but that some good can come from its ashes like a phoenix. 'Remembrance' is the process which makes this metamorphosis possible.

An amazing part of 'remembrance' is that you cannot remember Bahá'u'lláh while you dwell on the elements of the lower nature. 'Abdu'l-Bahá gave an example of this principle when He said, ' When your heart is filled with the love of God, there will not be room for sorrow, there will only be room for love and happiness' (V 110). 'Remembrance' automatically draws you up from your lower toward your higher nature. You cannot be thankful and depressed at the same time. Without 'remembrance' problems simply remain trouble without a guarantee of beneficial results. Reflection and consultation can reveal an endless number of practical ways to apply 'remembrance'.

The implications are obvious for the individual. They are equally important, though less apparent, in consultation.

If the consultative group is mainly interested in arbitrary authority or finding who is to blame while discussing a problem, little good is likely to result. However, if consultation is devoted to remembering Bahá'u'lláh by trying to create a healing or attempting to salvage good out of a bad situation, defilement is washed away.

Problem-solving through consultation

As the House of Justice has pointed out, problems may be taken to professional counselors, trusted friends or others involved with the matter. The Master said: '*Settle all things, both great and small, by consultation. Without prior consultation, take no important step in your own personal affairs. Concern yourselves with one another. Help along one another's projects and plans. Grieve over one another. Let none in the whole country go in need. Befriend one another until ye become as a single body, one and all . . .* (CC no. 20).

The Universal House of Justice points out that 'It should be borne in mind that all consultation is aimed at arriving at a solution to a problem and is quite different from the sort of group baring of the soul that is popular in some circles these days and which borders on the kind of confession that is forbidden in the Faith' (CC no. 47).

A believer can turn to his friends in time of need. One or several friends can be asked to meet for the purpose of consulting on some matter of concern. This is not a license to burden them with every little problem, but should be used as a serious search for solutions.

It is Bahá'í consultation when the purpose is to find a solution. It is *not* Bahá'í consultation when talking with others is for the purpose of gaining sympathy or finding a willing listener. It is not Bahá'í consultation when talking degenerates into a gripe session, or gossiping, or complaining. These activities, unlike Bahá'í consultation, increase both the problem and the hurt. Rather than 'letting the anger out' this process becomes a review and a rehearsal of the problem. It is dwelling on the unpleasant things of life. It causes delay, magnifies the hurt and interferes with any chance of a long-term improvement in the condition.

Consultation, on the other hand, seeks a solution and also has a soothing effect. The intensity of suffering is washed away by the '*living waters*' while a solution is developing. This is due both to the caring concern and the active steps being taken. It does not come from just talking about the situation.

There is something about being in the presence of loving friends who are eager to help that releases tension. Sharing of one's innermost concerns in consultation dissipates the anguish, the hurt or the fear which may be present. One who has borne troubles almost beyond endurance can find the strength, the perspective, the calm, the will to carry on: it can be the breath of life. New hope is discovered and a way out of a dilemma can be found.

Consultation illuminates three aspects of any question. These have to do with understanding and accepting (1) the problem, (2) the solution and (3) the consequences of that solution.

The true nature of the problem can be discovered most easily through consultation and can then be placed in its proper perspective. Sometimes the greatest frustration is not having a clear understanding of what the real problem is. Help in having that clarified can be a giant step toward acceptance. Psychologists have found that understanding is the most important single step in reducing anger.

Different courses of action can be examined, including that of taking no action. Then the most reasonable choice can be selected. Often a course of action is clear but there is difficulty in accepting it. Consultation can help a person accept what must be done. The best action may be to learn to live with a situation. Getting a 'just' solution may create a new problem which is worse than the original one. We all have limited and biased concepts of what is right. Insisting on a personal understanding of justice may cause more grief than accepting an injustice. Real help may come in the form of learning to accept the situation rather than going to great effort for the satisfaction of fulfilling one's own interpretation of justice.

The Guardian gave this advice in one situation. His secretary wrote in his behalf, 'Perhaps the greatest test Bahá'ís are ever subjected to is from each other; but for the sake of the Master they should be ever ready to overlook each other's mistakes, apologize for harsh words they have uttered, forgive and forget. He strongly recommends to you this course of action.' (December 18, 1945, LL 24). It is interesting that no reference was made to who was 'right' or what was 'just' or 'righting the wrong'.

Finally both the means and the courage to carry out the decision become available. The advice given by the Guardian in the above quotation may not be easy for some to follow. Loving consultation with friends can be a major step toward forgiving and forgetting so that a healing may begin.

In the long run the stress of the problem, cradled by consultation, produces new and wonderful insights and experiences which may actually be treasured long after the problem itself has been forgotten.

Consultation among friends is not binding. However, the results should be considered seriously because of the promise that divine assistance is available when consultation is carried out in the proper spirit.

Another significant source of assistance for consultation is the institution of the Learned. Any believer is free to turn to the Auxiliary Board member or assistant when facing a problem. There is a power and protection within that institution which is unique to this age. Often direct help is available in this manner. Sometimes other sources of help for a dilemma may be developed during consultation with a member of that wonderful institution.

Spiritual Assemblies and personal problems

Matters pertaining to the Faith should obviously be taken to the institutions concerned with the problem. It is also appropriate to take personal problems to one's own Spiritual Assembly. Within that divine creation there is a special guidance: a power to penetrate and touch the heart is found there which has no counterpart in the non-Bahá'í world. Healing, even of extremely difficult wounds, can take place under the loving concern of a sensitive Spiritual Assembly.

The Guardian gave one believer this advice:

. . . he feels that you should turn to your local Assembly, in the strictest confidence, and seek their aid and advice. These bodies have the sacred obligation to help, advise, protect and guide the believers in every way within their power when appealed to – indeed they were established just for the purpose of keeping order and unity and obedience to the law of God amongst the believers.

You should go to them [your local Assembly] as a child would to its parents . . . (LSA 16)

Another important consideration is that in a sense the Spiritual Assembly needs these problems for its own development, as the Guardian's secretary wrote on his behalf:

The Guardian wishes to emphasize the importance of avoiding [reference to civil courts] of cases of dispute between believers, even in non-Bahá'í issues. It is the Assembly's function to endeavor to settle amicably such disputes, both in order to safeguard the fair name and prestige of the Cause, and to acquire the necessary experience for the extension of its functions in the future. (DG no. 36)

No sooner had the Universal House of Justice called for greater development of Local Spiritual Assemblies than some communities were swamped with personal problems. This was part of their development and thus a bounty.

When a believer takes his problem to a Spiritual Assembly there is a strong two-edged obligation. On the one hand, the members of the Spiritual Assembly are under the injunction to have '*regard for the interests of the servants of God, for His sake, even as they regard their own interests, and to choose that which is meet and seemly*'. This is a responsibility before God. On the other hand, the individual is asking a divine institution to consider his problem and he had better be prepared to follow its advice. It may be very different from what he expects or wants.

In some very large communities the Spiritual Assembly may have many personal matters with which it must deal. It is sometimes necessary to have a special means of assistance with this work. If it is a committee or a delegation or an individual instead of the Assembly who meets with the believer, the protection and blessings of the divine institution are still present.

In small or new communities some believers may feel that the institution cannot handle the problem he or she wishes to present. But guidance from on high is promised to the Assembly, and it is available to new as well as old and experienced Spiritual Assemblies.

The members of the Spiritual Assembly must be mindful that they are dealing with wounded hearts which need to be healed. They are not simply trying to administer justice, find out who was at fault, establish restitution or deal only with 'administrative' aspects. The purpose is to bring about an understanding and a healing.

Feeling abandoned

There is an occasional situation in which one may be forced to seek answers alone; there is no other choice. It can be one of the saddest hours in the life of a Bahá'í when he is confronted with a personal crisis of overwhelming magnitude and there seems to be no one – individual or institution – to whom he can turn. He can be overcome by a feeling of loneliness, alienation or even abandonment which can be devastating. It can seem a dire calamity when the support is not there when needed. Yet it happens and will happen again.

The Faith is in its infancy. The institutions are not always functioning at the level to be desired. Further, Bahá'ís are few in number, sometimes busy with their own affairs and not always available in time of need. Being human, all have their own weaknesses, and inexperience with human problems may mean the available Bahá'ís are not as sensitive as they ought to be.

At such times some people have become angry at the Faith, at other believers or at the institutions for being unresponsive to their needs. Some are even angry at themselves for feeling so dependent. Too often people make tests more difficult because of impatience either with others or with themselves.

There is no guarantee in the Writings that we are going to be able to get help from one another when we need it most. The history of man and the history of the Cause are filled with episodes in which individuals were forced to draw their strength entirely from their own relationship with God. '*Be not grieved if thou performest it thyself alone. Let God be all-sufficient for thee*' (GL 280). We are working toward a world which will be more loving and responsive to the needs of others. We do not have it yet.

In a letter dated October 22, 1949, written on behalf of the Guardian to an individual believer, the following is stated:

We must be patient with others, infinitely patient! but also with our own poor selves, remembering that even the Prophets of God got tired and called out in despair! . . . He urges you to persevere and add up your accomplishments, rather than to dwell on the dark side of things. Everyone's life has both a dark side and a bright side. The Master said, ' *turn your back on the darkness and your face to me* '. (UD 456-7)

There is only one thing that will never fail; only one thing which can never be taken away: '*For every one of you his paramount duty is to choose for himself that on which no other may infringe and none usurp from him. Such a thing – and to this the Almighty is My witness – is the love of God, could ye but perceive it*' (GL 261). When this love is strong, it is possible to withstand whatever happens.

Sometimes it is in circumstances in which one seems to stand alone that the greatest inner and unexpected strength develops.

Consultation with one's self

Turning to one's own inner resources for guidance is always possible. This can be done in many ways: one is to simply think a problem through; another is to reflect on the matter in prayer.

Another form of personal problem-solving is through imaginary conversation with a trusted friend with whom you could consult if the person were available. Reduce the issue to its simplest terms so you can explain it to your friend. Sometimes it helps to write this out. During this process an answer sometimes becomes evident because a better understanding of the problem has been gained. Of course there is nothing wrong with writing to the friend. Consultation through the mail was highly recommended by the beloved Guardian. He consulted through the mail regularly.

Still another type of consultation is with one's own soul. In 'Abdu'l-Bahá's famed letter to the Swiss psychiatrist, Professor Forel, the following is found:

The mind is circumscribed, the soul limitless. It is by the aid of such senses as those of sight, hearing, taste, smell and touch, that the mind comprehendeth, whereas, the soul is free from all agencies. The soul as thou observest, whether it be in sleep or waking, is in motion and active. Possibly it may, whilst in a dream, unravel an intricate problem, incapable of solution in the waking state . . . the soul is ever endowed with full strength. (BWF 337-8)

This kind of consultation transfers the question from the conscious mind to the soul where marvelous answers are to be found. In some ways it resembles the process of decision-making in Chapter 3.

There are, however, some significant differences. After getting as clear a picture of the problem as possible, STOP thinking about it. The idea is to give the gist of the problem to the soul, using the faculty of inner vision and *not* to dwell on it with the conscious mind. It may take some practice to turn off the mind, but it can be done. One good way is to think about some other specific thing, task or problem not related to the matter being considered. Psychologists refer to this as the incubation period, that is, a time when there is no conscious effort at finding the solution. The soul has the capacity to work on it while you are asleep or absorbed in something else.

An answer will come. It may come in the middle of the night or in the midst of prayer, or while driving, walking, riding a bus or doing the dishes. Quite often it will come in a moment of relative solitude and quiet. It can also just slip into the middle of a conversation, come into focus from a chance remark or while watching television. It may come as a dramatic flash or just gradually become apparent.

This method was used often in the writing of this book. Many concepts which perplexed the mind became clarified through this process. Ideas about wording also appeared this way.

While this system produces excellent answers for individuals it is not a substitute for consultation with others. There are many situations in which the contributions and the interaction of others are preferable and, when feasible, should be used. It must also be remembered that answers received this way are not free from error. In fact, the answer may be crystal clear but faulty due to incomplete, erroneous or misunderstood facts. The faculty of inner vision cannot supply missing information, although often information is used which had been 'forgotten'. Twisted or distorted perceptions or preconceived notions may remain.

Under no circumstances should conclusions reached in this manner be imposed on others. It is for individual guidance only. Writing through his secretary on a closely related matter the Guardian said:

The questions you ask in your letter about individual guidance have two aspects, one might say. It is good that people should turn to God and beseech His aid in solving their problems and guiding their acts, indeed every day of their lives, if they feel the desire to do so. But they cannot possibly impose what they feel to be their guidance on anyone else, let alone on Assemblies or Committees, as Bahá'u'lláh has expressly laid down the law of consultation and never indicated that anything else superseded it. (CC no. 37)

Weigh any answers received in this way against these two questions: 1. Is the answer consistent with the Writings? 2. Will it hurt anything? If the answers are yes and no respectively, implement the solution with conviction, yet with caution. The caution should be used to review the answer to be sure it proves worthy in actual use. Sometimes when an answer comes it may seem definite; later, it may be discovered that the answer is faulty or only a temporary solution. It may be a necessary but incomplete step until a better solution is found or more information comes to light.

By the practiced use of this technique many wonderful answers can be found to otherwise perplexing questions.

Attitude towards others with problems
One of the true marks of spiritual maturity is seen in the attitude a person has about someone else who is going through a spiritual battle.

Society in general reflects anything from disdain through indifference to compassion to people with problems.

There are often two conflicting impulses. One is to offer the helping hand of compassion and understanding. The other, especially when the problem is the obvious result of wrongdoing, breaking a law, Bahá'í or civil, or simply poor judgment, is to think either in terms of punishment or that the person brought it on himself.

Fortunately, in the Bahá'í community there is no need for a conflict. There is an ideal arrangement in that society is protected from wrongdoers, punishment is given as required, yet the individual can still act with love, forgiveness and compassion.

Assemblies will one day be called Houses of Justice. They are not to be called houses of mercy. They have the responsibility to do justice before God for all mankind. Individuals, however, are to offer kindness, to soothe troubled hearts. They have the responsibility to report any wrongdoing to the proper institution, but their attitude as individuals should not be confused with their administrative responsibilities. Individual Bahá'ís must never try to act as Spiritual Assemblies to each other. Often it has happened that one believer, acting in behalf of an institution, will offer a stern reprimand to another believer. Later that same person will show the greatest personal compassion and understanding. The two roles are not contradictory; instead they reflect the fact that this is the age of maturity. Institutions must act with justice; the individual must act with love and forbearance.

In dealing with people who are experiencing severe personal problems one unwelcome feature is often present – anxiety. This can be expressed in apprehension, extreme uneasiness of mind or brooding fear: worry.

There are two serious ways in which anxiety makes consultation more difficult and interferes with the efforts of others to be helpful. One is an extreme sense of emergency and the other is irrationality.

EMERGENCY. There is often a distorted sense of the importance of the problem. The person wrestling with a question may well regard all details, no matter how trivial, as being of supreme importance. It is easy for others to be philosophical and say that tests make us grow and view each dilemma in perspective. Not so for the individual who is seized by the pain, the anguish and the pressure of anxiety.

Emotionally there is nothing to compare with crushing, all-consuming and sometimes paralyzing mental anguish. The level of stress becomes higher and higher. For those trying to help it means that time and gentleness, even when being firm, are of the essence. Delays, for whatever reason, intensify the hurt disproportionately. Additional slights and hurts become magnified. The paramount need is to reduce stress. Then attention can be focused on more basic issues.

IRRATIONALITY. Logic and reason lose their power when problems become emotional. Irrational and inconsistent thought and behavior are common and come with anxiety. Those trying to help may get discouraged because the one needing help may do more foolish things contrary to all the good advice he has been given. This is simply a symptom of stress and being anxious. It should not discourage or be taken as a reason to give up trying to help. The consequences of anxiety are reduced when there is loving support to reduce stress and give needed assistance.

The Writings are filled with admonitions to be compassionate and encouraging to those in need. However, care must be exercised so as not to meddle in other people's business. Sometimes the best help is to do nothing directly. To offer prayers, give support and help only when requested is still a positive step and may be the best assistance which can be given at that time.

Certain problems bring out feelings of sympathy, but there are others which create feelings of repulsion. People may need help whether their problem is one which attracts sympathy or one that repels. It takes a special measure of true Bahá'í character to continue offering support to people experiencing the kinds of problems which, by their very nature, are repulsive.

When problems involve disobedience to Bahá'í laws and teachings another complication arises. There are no perfect Bahá'ís. Still, many are shocked when a well-known Bahá'í does something which is clearly wrong.

A believer might find himself in the unusual position of being surrounded by several others who are disregarding Bahá'í law. It can be an enormous test for someone who wants to do the right thing to see others act with a seemingly careless attitude toward Bahá'í law. The more open and flagrant the disobedience, the greater the test for those who are trying to be obedient. What should a believer do in such a situation?

Bahá'u'lláh gives us the necessary guidance for developing the proper attitude toward those breaking the laws:

If ye meet the abased or the down-trodden, turn not away disdainfully from them, for the King of Glory ever watcheth over them and surroundeth them with such tenderness as none can fathom except them that have suffered their wishes and desires to be merged in the Will of your Lord, the Gracious, the All-Wise . . . Blessed are the learned that pride not themselves on their attainments; and well is it with the righteous that mock not the sinful, but rather conceal their misdeeds, so that their own shortcomings may remain veiled to men's eyes. (GL 314–15)

Next, do not weaken even if you seem to be the only one in your area trying to live by the healing message of the Divine Physician. Do not let others pull you down. There are thousands throughout the world just as conscientious. Many of the martyrs achieved the crown of martyrdom because of their high moral standards. In flagrant cases report the activity to a responsible institution such as a Spiritual Assembly or an Auxiliary Board member or his assistant. This is not backbiting or gossiping. It enables the person to get rid of the problem by dealing with it in the proper manner.

When in doubt about how to deal with personal problems, there is no substitute for consultation. A reasonable course of action can generally be discovered.

Tests are not only a natural part of life but necessary. The Master said: '*Life is a load which must be carried on . . .*' (PT 99). This implies that there are more tests to come! When they *do* come they must be dealt with. Some of the same principles apply whether it is a test for the individual or affects the Bahá'í community as a whole, whether it is being handled by an individual or through a consultative group. Here are some specific suggestions which can help:

1. Try to place the problem in its proper perspective and view it objectively, both in terms of its importance and in terms of time.
2. Look for and concentrate on any good features which may be present.
3. Try to discover any lessons from the experience which can be of value.

4. Find ideas for a solution. Often the key to the best way of handling a problem is suggested in the question itself. It may or may not be obvious. Generally solutions will emerge with consultation and a careful search.

5. Redirecting thoughts helps. For example, many people find sitting in a dentist's chair a source of stress. If at that time, thoughts are directed into prayer or trying to figure out some way to teach the Faith more effectively, two things will happen. First of all, the immediate tension will be reduced. Secondly, some fascinating ideas for teaching may develop. One inspiration which opened up a whole new area to the Faith had its origin in a dentist's chair.

6. Whenever possible, turn the matter around so that it becomes an advantage.

Perhaps the best single example of how opposition can be turned around and used to an advantage came from the pen of the beloved Guardian. When there was an attack on the Will and Testament of 'Abdu'l-Bahá he took the occasion to write to the believers of the West. In his letter of clarification he said of the opposition:

We should feel truly thankful for such futile attempts to undermine our beloved Faith – attempts that protrude their ugly face from time to time, seem for a while able to create a breach in the ranks of the faithful, recede finally into the obscurity of oblivion, and are thought of no more. Such incidents we should regard as the interpositions of Providence, designed to fortify our faith, to clarify our vision and to deepen our understanding of the essentials of His Divine Revelation. (WOB 3)

The Guardian then proceeded, over the next several years, to 'fortify our faith', 'clarify our vision', and 'deepen our understanding' by a series of letters now collected in the book entitled *The World Order of Bahá'u'lláh*. How ironic that a futile attempt at opposition, at destroying the Cause of God, became the opportunity for the first stage of giving to the entire Bahá'í world such a clear outline of the essential verities of the Faith and a keener understanding of its divine purpose!

This example demonstrates how a challenge can be seized and used as a step toward progress. The real test is to use every situation in such a way that it can further the best interests of the Cause. Doing so is a true fulfillment of what it means to be a servant of the Beloved in this glorious Day.

ELEVEN

Challenges to Unity

Nothing whatever can, in this Day, inflict a greater harm upon this Cause than dissension and strife, contention, estrangement and apathy, among the loved ones of God. Flee them, through the power of God and His sovereign aid, and strive ye to knit together the hearts of men, in His Name, the Unifier, the All-Knowing, the All-Wise. (GL 9)

It is for good reason that conscientious Bahá'ís fear disunity in the community of the Greatest Name more than just about any other single thing. Nothing else stops the teaching work, stifles the spirit or produces so many problems as quickly as contention amongst the loved ones.

When everyone's vision is on the sublime majesty of the Ancient Beauty, the protective blessings of the Covenant and the noble tasks we are all called on to perform, there is no room for disunity. However, sometimes that vision slips and we face one another in all the rawness of our human nature. This is when problems begin.

Each person has his unique personality and a spiritual potential. In order to develop those divine possibilities, it is necessary for some of the raw edges of the personality to be removed. This is done through our dealings with one another; in this way each one becomes spiritually polished and refined. To achieve this we were given a world which needs improving. Better yet, we have a Bahá'í community within which to work. Therein can be found all the challenges any soul requires.

Disunity is the condition of a spiritual low point. Elevating vision and bringing the community to a point of affinity is challenging and rewarding and contributes to the fulfillment of life. In order to better understand this it is necessary to look at some of those human characteristics which, when out of touch with spiritual realities, lead to contention and serious problems.

Common Annoyances

'There are two kinds of Bahá'ís who are a great test to each other,' said a well-known traveling teacher while waiting for the two other members of the party to catch up, 'fast people and slow people.' Whether walking down the street, sharing a meal or trying to figure out how something works, the fast and the slow can present each other with serious problems. A quick-witted person may immediately see the main point, together with many of its implications and applications, as self-evident. The slower-thinking one may not be able to handle a sudden burst of thought; he needs time to understand even the first part of the issue. The quick thinker may become impatient and contemptuous of the person who is slow in figuring something out. The slower-thinking person may grow suspicious and critical of the one who races ahead. He may feel, because of his uneasy feeling of not quite understanding all that is happening, that the faster-thinking one is trying to slip something past him. One is not necessarily more creative than the other nor is one more thorough than the other. They are simply different and think at different speeds. Neither is superior to the other, but they are a severe test for each other.

Another set of different personalities which can cause difficulty is the practical and deliberate person in contrast with the impulsive and impetuous one. The practical person may view the other as going off half-cocked, whereas the impulsive one may be concerned that the more practical person works only with the head and never with the heart.

Two other types who create problems for each other are the energetic soul who wants to get everything done immediately and the phlegmatic person who never seems to have a sense of urgency about anything. A related pair consists of a person with an intense power of concentration trying to consult with an individual who has a short attention span and is easily distracted. The fact that the one can seem to go on and on without stopping can make others most uncomfortable. On the other hand, fidgety people can turn the more contemplative person into a nervous wreck.

Sometimes seated at the same conference table are a person who is a high achiever and someone who has difficulty coping with life. The one may be able to keep his personal and business affairs in good order and find opportunity and advantage in every problem. The other finds that nothing seems to work out well and rushes headlong from crisis to crisis; survival itself is looked upon as an accomplishment. Other than their love for Bahá'u'lláh, the only thing thay have in common is that each finds the life-style of the other completely incomprehensible.

A major challenge occurs when one with expansive vision and an eye for opportunity consults with those with more limited vision. There are those who, with purity of purpose but little understanding, undermine and discourage noble ventures. They condemn all they do not understand and they understand little.

Incompetence and easy promises are hard to accept for a person whose word is his bond and who does what he says. Yet seated with him may be one who volunteers for everything while accomplishing little, the secretary who fails to get the letters written or the treasurer who does not get the contributions forwarded.

Then there is the indecisive and halting individual who even after making a decision vacillates and wonders if it was the right one. The oriented and assured person, who makes a decision and then goes on to the next question, can easily become annoyed when the indecisive one wants to rehash issues which have already been settled. There are also some people who have difficulty in resolving issues. They invariably find some lingering unresolved threads and often attempt to reopen an item on the agenda. Their opposite wants to settle the issue with or without full and frank consultation and examination of all the facts. Making a decision becomes more important than the decision being right. Some people are flexible and adaptable and can adjust to any situation. Others are rigid and, once a course of action is set, will not change. There are those who feel secure with the way things have always been and are hesitant to try anything new. They sometimes try to consult with those who are ready to scrap anything that has already been done and are only excited by something because it is new, different and untried.

There is also the long-time Bahá'í who is set in his ways. He may know the Writings well. He may have served with distinction in some extremely difficult situations and performed great service for the Faith. Yet he may oppose every new idea and view bold projects with great skepticism.

What about people who seem to live on a high plane of intensity? That is, those who feel so strongly about something that it becomes an obsession. They have an intense sincerity; neither the motive nor the value of the project are questioned, but the intensity of feeling may make it difficult to see things in proper perspective and may alienate others.

There is also the stubborn one who never gives up an idea, or the one, easily persuaded, who agrees to anything, but sticks to nothing. There is the chronic complainer, the pessimist who sees only problems and the dark side of things. There is also the dreamer, the impractical and the naively optimistic who has no solutions and takes no action but is sure everything will turn out all right.

There are some who want to stop everything in order to evaluate the effectiveness of what has been done, in contrast with the one who feels that every detail that happens is the Will of God and 'the way it is supposed to be'. Then there are those who see the whole picture next to those who can only focus on one specific detail at a time.

There is also the glib problem-solver who has a quick answer to everyone else's dilemma, or the one who knows it all: no matter what the topic, he has a slick comment to make.

And the list could go on and on and on . . .

The Bahá'í community is made out of whole cloth. Every conceivable human characteristic – strength and weakness – is found among the followers of Bahá'u'lláh. Also, there is no end to the list of human characteristics that can become a source of irritation. Everyone has mannerisms which someone else considers a fault. Some people have a great tolerance for personal idiosyncrasies in others and some do not. Any and all possible combinations of irritating habits may be found within a Bahá'í community.

In this regard there is an interesting paradox:

1. It is easier to see faults in others than it is in ourselves.
2. It is easier to change our own behavior than it is to change the behavior of others.

In the Bahá'í community there is no way to escape some of the problems which arise as a result of different personalities, but discord cannot be allowed to linger. If it does, the community becomes side-tracked from its noble mission.

Giving up prejudices of skin color, race and national or religious origin, difficult though it may be, is easy compared to giving up the prejudices against those whose thoughts, values, traditions, habits, style, cultural or personal priorities are different. Therein lies a challenge which the Bahá'í community as a whole is just beginning to notice. It can be dealt with effectively through consultation.

Enduring Inefficiency

When a Spiritual Assembly does not function smoothly a special kind of test is created. One prominent believer who had years of experience working with Bahá'ís throughout the world knew the love and the capacity of the friends. He also knew that sometimes the work of the Cause was made more difficult than necessary because instructions were not always carried out very well.

One day he greeted a large gathering of Bahá'ís with these words: 'Oceans and oceans of love and mountains and mountains of inefficiency.'

Few assemblies of this day have reached a high degree of efficiency, either in consultation or in carrying out plans. This is a real and serious frustration for those believers for whom a high level of personal achievement is normal. For them consultation can sometimes seem a great waste of time. Those whose work habits are concentrated and intense with clear objectives may find the slower paced, sometimes rambling and inefficient assembly or committee meetings extremely difficult. It is worse when some of the comments made during consultation are patently illogical or disjointed and sometimes ludicrous. Problems are aggravated by a chairman, secretary, treasurer or other key person who may be incompetent or ineffective. Muddling through the mistakes and ineptitude of others can drain the joy from any task. Boredom, being 'turned-off', becoming nervous or fidgety or even disgusted and angry are predictable symptoms. In addition the frustration of decisions not being carried out in a timely manner can become almost unbearable. A martyr's path may seem preferable to the stumbling, fumbling and bumbling which goes on sometimes. 'What am I doing here?' 'Who needs this?', achievement-oriented individuals may seriously ask themselves. 'I have more important things to do with my time', or, 'There are better ways to serve the Faith!' may be exasperated conclusions.

Finding reasons to miss meetings can easily be the result. 'I've been too busy' might be the excuse when, in fact, it is because the meetings are unrewarding. The lure of other more pleasant, gratifying and seemingly more productive activities becomes increasingly appealing. Even noble-sounding schemes of service to the Cause can be contrived as an alternative to enduring a committee or assembly meeting which has become tedious. Rising above these sources of frustration takes enormous strength, faith and self-discipline.

It should not be too surprising that the work of the Faith is sometimes performed in a less than ideal manner. Some of those called upon to do the work of the Cause have no background, training or experience for their sacred tasks. Some lack confidence or necessary skills. Many believers with unsure feet and unclear vision are very much involved and play a notable role in the divine drama.

This Cause – this ark of salvation for all mankind – must pass through these early perilous times, revealing uneven growth and development along the way. The Guardian explained to an individual believer: 'We should view the Cause in the light of a perfect system, operating as yet through very imperfect instruments. Gradually, through the deepening of individual spiritual consciousness and general change the world itself must undergo, the perfection of this will become manifest and fully operative' (WO July 1943, 115).

Reflecting on that thought it becomes obvious that no useful purpose is served by indulging in wishful thinking about more qualified people, dwelling on each other's imperfections, dreaming about other ways of serving the Faith or how to escape from the inadequacies of the moment.

One must serve the assembly or committee of which one is a part, not the glories of a non-existent one based on imagination of what 'should be'. Where there are problems they must be viewed in the context of present conditions. Then a definite purpose is served by consulting openly and frankly about the situation.

Internal difficulties should be resolved within the consultative group itself if at all possible. If problems cannot be resolved, assistance should be requested. Committees can turn to their Spiritual Assemblies for help. Local Spiritual Assemblies can request aid from their Auxiliary Board or guidance from the National Spiritual Assembly, which in turn can receive the benefit of counsel from the Continental Board of Counsellors or the Universal House of Justice. There is more on this in Chapter 13.

If a problem involves the functioning of one or more of the officers, steps must be taken to be sure the necessary duties are carried out in some manner. Details will vary depending on the circumstances. It is necessary either to overcome or work around the difficulties.

The fact is that although a great number of people are ill-suited for the duties they must perform, nonetheless, the jobs need to be done. If there are no qualified people to do these things, someone else must often do the best he can. For the individual it means doing what *must* be done instead of doing that for which he is best suited, or would prefer. It is an easy but inappropriate thing to say, 'Oh, I can't do that', and let it go. The beloved Guardian made this revealing distinction early in his ministry when he said: 'The time has come for the friends . . . to think not as to how they should serve the Cause, but how the Cause should be served' (PP 74). Surprising new talents and sources of strength have often been discovered when someone simply did what was needed.

We are promised '. . . that if we arise to play nobly our part every deficiency in our lives will be more than compensated by the all-conquering Spirit of His grace and power' (BA 88). That does not mean a dim-witted person will suddenly become brilliant or that a forgetful person will all of the sudden have a great memory, or that incompetence will magically change into competence, or that a difficult personality will be suddenly easy to get along with. It does mean there will be compensations. Something of benefit will happen. The compensation may be unrelated to the task on hand. God makes surprising use of the material available. All we have to do is 'play nobly our part' and be astonished by the compensations.

In the meantime, it is sometimes necessary to endure patiently the awkward conditions of inefficiency and ineptitude. While each one hopes, prays and strives for improvements, change does not always come swiftly. It is important to keep one's vision focused on the glorious potential of the institutions. The manifest difficulties of the moment must not be allowed to dim that vision. Perspective is renewed by recalling that the institutions are maturing and improving. There is a protection from on high which, in the long run, carries the institutions far, far, far beyond human limitations. This is the Cause of God. A safe journey is divinely ordained.

Bahá'u'lláh is bringing about a new civilization. Even the best and most efficient parts of existing systems are not equal to the job of creating a new world, otherwise a new system would not be necessary. Highly efficient, smoothly-running assemblies are certainly worthy. However, even those which make good decisions easily and quickly and 'get things done' are not doing their jobs unless there is active teaching and an atmosphere of love and harmony.

In order to perfect this God-given system, it is sometimes necessary for the individual to sacrifice talents, qualities, and preferences which he holds dear, and simply do that which needs to be done. The inconveniences and unpleasantness produced by a world in transition must be endured. They will eventually pass.

When competent and talented believers drift to other, more appealing activities it is really a great loss and tragedy which causes unnecessary set-backs. It is a type of abandonment of the institutions in time of need and hampers the natural development. Also, the individual is taking a serious step in regard to his own spiritual development, even though he may honestly think 'they don't need me'; or 'there is nothing more I can do'; or 'this is a waste of my time'. Those ideas are short-sighted and miss the real issue.

The inaction of a Bahá'í – for whatever reason – deprives the Cause of one unit of the motive power necessary to propel it towards its ultimate destiny. It robs the institutions of the very ingredient needed most – spiritually oriented and disciplined talent – for the speedy fulfillment of its divine potential.

What is really happening, as believers grope with the myriad problems of the committees and assemblies on which they serve, is a metamorphosis: the gradual changing from the old methods of operation to the system of the Blessed Beauty. The individual who perseveres, endures patiently, and willingly tolerates less than ideal consultation becomes the instrument through which that metamorphosis is possible. It is an extraordinarily high and noble form of service and sacrifice. The change that results comes about in slow, small, often repetitious and sometimes painful increments. That is the price paid for living in this age of transition.

In this process institutions slowly and mysteriously mature to achieve wonderful results, because they are under the special protection and bounty of the Blessed Beauty Himself. It is also because willing and capable souls persevered, even when they would rather be doing something else.

Attitudes toward Success

One ironic, but common, area in which problems occur has to do with success, both one's own and that of others. The Bahá'í Writings provide an extremely high standard for the conduct of affairs, both personal affairs and activities in the Faith. There is great encouragement to excel in all endeavors, to achieve excellence in all things.

Some of the friends think the idea of trying to excel creates a conflict with being a good Bahá'í. They seem to feel that the teachings on social justice imply the kind of equality in which everyone is the same.

Every soul is worthy, but all are different and have unique contributions to make. We differ greatly in our innate characteristics such as intelligence, talents and physical abilities. 'Abdu'l-Bahá confirmed this when He said: *'Difference of capacity in human individuals is fundamental. It is impossible for all to be alike, all to be equal, all to be wise'* (PUP 217). He also said that among mankind there were differences of station (SAQ 130). Some believers find this a difficult concept to accept as it seems to contradict the ideas of equality and brotherhood.

There is another area of possible confusion. The teachings exhort Bahá'ís to humility, self-denial, not asserting oneself over others and thinking of others as higher than oneself. Superficially, these virtues seem contrary to a quest for achievement, success and excellence.

Some believers may be content with mediocrity under the mistaken notion that striving for excellence is a selfish desire and would place them above others. Some even feel guilty about personal achievements, thinking they are not showing proper humility.

This question was clarified when 'Abdu'l-Bahá was in New York. He was asked: 'If a man has a superior intellect, should he come down to the station of those who are less capable?' His answer was extremely interesting:

Capacity and privilege in this Cause are intrinsic. Whosoever has a greater power of speech, whosoever has a greater power of attraction, whosoever has a greater sincerity, will advance, no matter what happens . . . It is true that all souls are not equal. Some souls are in high stations of exaltation, – in the vanguard of the army; some are in the second rank. This is an innate Cause. The friends of God must have utmost consideration for those souls who are sincere and endeavoring to serve in the Cause.

For example, when we see a man doing public service, we must have consideration for him; if he gives a good address, we must praise him; if he makes wise suggestions, and if good intentions appear from him, we must have for him the greatest consideration . . . Those who are distinguished among the friends must receive due consideration . . . Distinction is good – all distinctions are good – distinction of intellect – distinction of sincerity – all; because distinction means development.

He was then asked, 'Is not distinction dangerous for the individual?' To which he replied, '(laughingly), *All people are in danger. Man, in whatsoever degree he chances to be, is in danger. Can you single out a man who is beyond danger?'* (sw iii, no. 10, p. 8).

In a compilation published by the Universal House of Justice entitled *Excellence in All Things*, the following words of 'Abdu'l-Bahá are quoted; '*choose for yourselves a noble goal . . .*' (SWAB 35). '*Make ye then a mighty effort . . . that in every kind of excellence the people of God shall surpass all other human beings*' (SWAB 150). A prayer is found which requests '*successful outcomes in all things*'. '*I desire distinction for you*' is a specific admonition by the Master, as is the injunction to '*set a high example*'. In no uncertain terms Bahá'u'lláh told His followers to '*Vie ye with each other in the service of God and of His Cause. This is indeed what profiteth you in this world, and in that which is to come*' (ADJ 70).

Competing with others and excelling is clearly not a bad thing. Looking down on others is. That is where the subtle, but important, difference lies!

Personal achievement

Two major principles may be borne in mind in attaining personal success without allowing one's achievements themselves to become a problem. One is giving credit where it is due. The other is the ability to maintain the proper sense of proportion.

CREDIT. In a very real sense Bahá'ís can always say, 'It was Bahá'u'lláh', whenever there is a successful venture. In addition to the general idea that everything is done for Him there are two other reasons why this is true.

1. Everything one does is based on some natural talent or ability. This is a gift from God. No one can take credit for the natural talent with which he was born; that credit rightfully belongs to God.

2. The Writings say we should strive for worthy goals, to develop talents and achieve excellence. Therefore by following the instructions superior achievement results. That means even the credit for achievement really belongs to God. Individually we are the vessels in which God-given talents can develop.

By knowing where the credit really belongs, it is possible to enjoy success without being consumed by it.

PROPORTION. One of the Hands of the Cause was standing facing the sun with some other Bahá'ís to have a picture taken. Someone started to praise him, whereupon he took one step forward and said, 'Now, can I say I am any closer to the sun than you are?' Without denying his achievements or his station, he immediately placed the whole matter in its proper perspective.

Success is simply another test which must be overcome. The key is not to lose perspective. At least thirty-six Hands of the Cause have been appointed during their own lifetimes, and their appointments were indeed high praise for those precious souls. Yet of these only one, C. Mason Remey, was so overcome with self-importance that he violated the Covenant and removed himself from its protection. The others kept their vision and sense of proportion.

It is all right to excel. It is all right to try things and do well. It is all right to praise and congratulate others when they do well. It is all right to feel good about accomplishments. It is all right to appreciate congratulations from others when something has been done well. What is not all right is to glory in the praise and adulation or allow it to go to the head.

Bahá'ís should work for success and high attainments in all undertakings. Success does not stand in opposition to humility. It is a fulfillment when the attitude is right. Success does provide another spiritual struggle, but of this the Guardian said:

If we could perceive the true reality of things we would see that the greatest of all battles raging in the world today is the spiritual battle. If the believers like yourself, young and eager and full of life, desire to win laurels for true and undying heroism, then let them join in the spiritual battle – whatever their physical occupation may be – which involves the very soul of man. The hardest and the noblest task in the world today is to be a *true* Bahá'í; this requires that we defeat not only the current evils prevailing all over the world, but the weaknesses, attachments to the past, prejudices, and selfishnesses that may be inherited and acquired within our own characters; that we give forth a shining and incorruptible example to our fellow-men. *(From a letter dated April 5, 1942, to an individual believer.)*

Success of others

When anyone accomplishes anything of significance either personally or for the Cause, or when one works especially hard, there is always the danger that someone else will try to belittle it. The greater the accomplishment or the more work done, the louder and more conspicuous the chorus of those who would negate it. Of these detractors 'Abdu'l-Bahá said: '. . . *they cannot withstand the very first test – that of rejoicing over the success of their neighbor, at which God rejoices. Only by such a sincere joy can the gift of God descend unto a pure heart*' (sw vi, 44).

Sometimes appreciation or congratulations are withheld because of the fear of 'exalting' someone. Sometimes obstacles are thrown in someone's way because of a sincere but inappropriate fear that that person may become self-aggrandizing. Sometimes there is a tendency to minimize what others accomplish.

The human spirit can be compared to a beautiful butterfly. When bathed in the warm sunshine of encouragement it will soar and swoop to everyone's delight. But it is delicate and fragile. It can easily be stepped on and crushed so that it lies lifeless in the dust, crumpled and shorn of its beauty. The Master quoted lovely verses cautioning us not to harm our fellow human beings:

> *Unless ye must,*
> *Bruise not the serpent in the dust,*
> *How much less wound a man.*
> *And if ye can,*
> *No ant should ye alarm.*
> *Much less a brother harm.* (SWAB 256)

And if the Master advocated such sensitivity to the serpent and the ant, should we not be even more sensitive to the 'butterflies' of each other's human spirits? – please be careful of each other's butterflies.

Among the characteristics of highly talented and effective people are a high level of activity and singleness of purpose. To others this is sometimes misinterpreted as an obsession with reaching objectives at any cost.

A person of conventional vision working closely with the highly talented one faces great frustration. If he does not understand the other there may be mistrust and an attempt to keep things from happening quite so fast. Much effort can be consumed trying to slow down a project, just because things are happening faster than can be easily understood.

One of the real tests for the person of talent and imagination is to remain strong when others question his intentions, motives and integrity. With misguided self-righteousness, less gifted people can undermine efforts, allow secondary matters to take on exaggerated importance and retard progress. 'Abdu'l-Bahá said:

When God calls a soul to a high station, it is because that soul has capacity for that station as a gift of God, and because that soul has supplicated to be taken into His service. No envies, jealousies, calumnies, slanders, plots, nor schemes, will ever move God to remove a soul from its intended place, for by the grace of God, such actions on the part of the people are the test of the servant, testing his strength, forbearance, endurance and sincerity under adversity. (sw vi, 44)

The implications for consultation are enormous. Many a brilliant project has been squashed, not because it was ill-conceived or mis-directed, but because those with limited vision smothered the creative spark. The progress of the Faith itself can be slowed down and the spirit of loving service and enterprise dies. Too many talented believers have been discouraged and turned away from Bahá'í activi-ties. They then direct their energies into other activities which they find more rewarding. On the other hand, many who do not catch on to what is going on give up in frustration because it may look as if someone is trying to run everything, or they just do not know what to do. Wise counsel and leadership, through consultation, must use the talents both of the highly gifted and those of more limited vision. Everyone's talents are needed. It is a challenge, but one that consulta-tion can easily meet.

In the *Tablets of the Divine Plan* 'Abdu'l-Bahá described an awesome event. Speaking of those souls who comprise the '*heavenly armies*', He said:

Should one of them turn his face toward some direction and summon the people to the Kingdom of God, all the ideal forces and lordly confirmations will rush to his support and reinforcement. He will behold all the doors open and all the strong fortifications and impregnable castles razed to the ground. Singly and alone he will attack the armies of the world, defeat the right and left wings of the hosts of all the nations and carry his attack to the very center of the powers of the earth. This is the meaning of the Hosts of God. (TDP 47–8)

This breathtaking account suggests vigorous, charismatic, effective individual leadership. It also implies a multitude of problems which are bound to develop. There are a great many Bahá'ís who would be terrified if such a thing were to start in their community. With self-righteous indignation they would try to use consultation to tone down or try to stop those very events described by the pen of the Master. Then there is a danger that those institutions not prepared to support and accept such startling activities would find themselves in opposition to the onward march of the Cause of God. The event described is not to be taken lightly. The Center of the Covenant wrote it. It will happen. And it may not be recognized as a divine bounty when it occurs.

Energetic and single-minded determination to serve the Cause can be unsettling. How would some of today's Spiritual Assemblies react to the kind of zeal displayed by the Dawn-Breakers? Would a Táhirih, Mullá Husayn, Quddús or Hujjat get support from fellow-believers or would they be told to slow down and be more patient, to take it easy?

When a person's vision of the Cause stops growing there follows complacency and a tendency to limit activity to a level which is comfortable. A complacent person finds it disturbing when others want to do more. The result may be frustration or attempts to slow down the others.

No human can fully apprehend the glory, the majesty, the scope of this great Cause. Only as vision expands can creative energies latent in individual believers become ignited and be channeled into service. It is a never-ending but essential challenge to keep one's vision expanding. As the beloved Guardian said: 'To strive to obtain a more adequate understanding of the significance of Bahá'u'lláh's stupendous Revelation must, it is my unalterable conviction, remain the first obligation and the object of the constant endeavor of each of its loyal adherents' (WOB 100). Unchecked by constructive consultation, limited vision and all its cousins squash creativity, frustrate individual initiative and inhibit personal achievement.

But consultation makes it possible to analyze situations and place aspects in their proper perspective. It aids people to rise above petty grievances and concerns. Then the ideal forces, greater illumination, support and encouragement propel the Cause of God forward with everyone's 'butterfly' intact.

Conflicting Feelings

One of the seven prerequisites for those who take counsel together is purity of motive. 'Abdu'l-Bahá over and over again encouraged the believers to purify the motives of their hearts. Probably one of the reasons why this is stressed is that no one is really pure.

Generally speaking, Bahá'ís are more free from ulterior motives than others. However, hidden purposes can subtly enter into consultation. Many of these desires are not at all sinister.

Some ulterior motives may be as simple as wanting to be sure that the meeting is over by ten o'clock so as to be able to get home to get a good night's sleep before going to work the next day, or to get home in time to watch a television show of particular interest, or even because of some prearranged teaching.

When something comes on the agenda that looks as though it may be long and drawn out and the time to leave is fast approaching, there may be a tendency to try to cut consultation short in order to get out on time. Motives become mixed. The result is indecision or arbitrary answers which are not thought through.

There is a more honest way to deal with the matter. Discuss it. Simply say you would like to be done by such and such a time. Then determine whether or not it is best to proceed with the consultation, postpone it, have yourself excused, forgo your other activity, or handle it in some other manner. In other words, rather than dealing with mixed motives and vacillation it is better to state the real problem, which is a conflict of interests. It is a little like trying to read with a dripping faucet in the background. The harder one tries to concentrate, the louder the faucet seems to get. Fixing the faucet before going back to reading can save a lot of time and frustration. The same principle applies to mixed feelings. Deal with them: they will not solve themselves. Then the consultation will not be influenced by motives not shared by others.

When there are mixed motives and conflicting feelings consultation suffers. A feeling develops of being rushed or cut short. There is a vague uneasiness, an apprehensive feeling that things were not done quite the way they should have been.

It is not possible to eliminate all mixed motives. In fact, it is not even possible to identify all the conflicting feelings everyone has. Nor is it even worthwhile to try to figure out all the possible conflicting motives. However, to the degree that they interfere with consultation, preoccupations should be examined, dealt with and set aside.

When there is a feeling of preoccupation or of mixed motives it is desirable to mention it. A simple statement like, 'There is something going on here that I don't understand', can cause the group to stop, take a look at itself and, perhaps, resolve the problem.

Mixed emotions are another common element. Human beings are extremely complex; joy and sorrow frequently embrace in a single occurrence. A decision may be made to forge ahead into new activities and there is a joy and certain enthusiasm about that. There may also be apprehension and fear of venturing into the unknown. Hence more vacillating.

Mixed emotions, which accompany nearly every element of consultation, must be accepted for what they are. There is no need to feel guilty about them. They are natural and provide a part of the richness and the balance of life.

In everyday life many things are greeted with mixed feelings. Why should consultation be free of them? When this simple fact is recognized it is easier to deal with the consequences of conflicting feelings without being torn by them. Many people have legitimate conflicting feelings about many issues but do not recognize them nor accept this conflict as being all right. Consultation can help illuminate those concerns and lay them aside. Unfounded fears can be dissipated; unrealistic hopes and aims can be seen for what they are. When 'joy and sorrow embrace' inseparably consultation can help people accept that fact.

To summarize, both mixed emotions and mixed motives are real and vital parts of life and they cause conflict. Rather than pretending they do not exist, the impact each makes should be examined honestly and openly in consultation when appropriate. In this way a normal part of life does not disrupt, but rather enriches consultation and vacillating can be minimized.

TWELVE

Serious Disturbances

In addition to the common annoyances of life there are some problems whose presence in a Bahá'í community can put a severe strain on amity and accord. They are often more difficult to deal with because they involve situations in which one or more persons are unable or unwilling to promote unity, or are not interested in doing so. The solution is not as simple as everyone refocusing his vision and rising above petty grievance.

Emotional Problems

Occasionally an assembly may find a situation where consultation is impossible because of an emotional problem. This may affect a specific issue such as two members of the assembly going through a divorce or a personal dispute filled with turmoil. It may be a larger, more pervasive problem. A person may be facing a crisis or even a series of crises in life which have an inordinate impact on emotional strength. There may be a situation of senility or some other serious mental disorder in which it is simply not within a person's capacity to deal rationally or effectively with many issues.

At times such emotional problems result in loud, boisterous, and sometimes crude interruptions or outbursts at a Feast or perhaps an assembly meeting. The outburst must not be allowed to continue. If it is in an assembly meeting, stop consultation until a more propitious time. If it happens at a Feast or other meeting, the one creating the disturbance must be firmly but lovingly stopped or removed from the situation. Then try to regain normalcy and forget about the outburst.

If nothing else works, it may be necessary to end the meeting with the hope of having a more uplifting one next time. Naturally, the Spiritual Assembly must deal with this at its next meeting.

If repeated attempts on the part of the assembly to deal with the matter have been futile, the problem must be referred to an Auxiliary Board member or assistant or to the National Spiritual Assembly or appropriate committee. There are several actions which can be taken by other institutions. In the meantime, how does a community cope with such emotional problems?

One way is to learn to live with it. This is not easy; indeed, it may be the greatest challenge in the entire experience of the Bahá'ís involved. The attitude must be loving and patient no matter what. Sometimes the situation is such that it brings out the most unloving and impatient qualities in people. That is a great test and must be faced. It may help to think how the one causing the problems must be suffering. That poor soul must live with himself all the time and is probably miserable. Remembering that makes it easier to endure a few unpleasant hours.

It may also help to think of those causing the disruption as children or relatives with severe handicaps. That, in fact, is the case. The handicap is the inability to communicate effectively. Yet one does not abandon a child or close relative just because of a severe problem and the fact that coping with the situation is difficult.

The value to the one enduring this kind of experience may go far beyond the immediate problem. Learning patience and long-suffering in a situation where no solution seems possible may well prepare those involved for future service in which that quality, because it was developed, may be the key to handling some important and delicate matter affecting the Cause.

Confrontations

Sometimes an individual may choose to have a confrontation with a Spiritual Assembly in the form of an ultimatum such as 'Am I right or wrong?' The question involved is usually not so simple as that. However, the one doing the confronting does not seem to be able to assimilate the idea of consultation or the fact that other choices may be more appropriate.

This may be caused by spiritual immaturity, insecurity or insincerity. A tendency to confront a Spiritual Assembly with an expectancy of a simple and immediate 'right or wrong' answer may also come from a person who is rigid in his thinking, intense or a compulsive personality. These individuals may have little tolerance for the suspended decisions which are required in consultation as solutions shape.

This condition may be because consultation is a new and unfamiliar form of decision-making. It may also result from an especially emotion-laden topic or situation. Or it may be pathological. The individual may not be ready to accept advice from others. He may be incapable of accepting the possibility that he may be wrong. It may be a defensive barrier to protect his own fragile self-concept. Often, the best way to deal with the situation is lovingly and with patience. Try to nurture the individual to a better understanding so he can more easily accept counsel.

For the normal sincere individual the capacity for suspended judgments will increase as he becomes accustomed to and comfortable with the process of evolving decisions through consultation. When this reaction is from an emotional situation the need for a quick answer will disappear as anxiety is reduced. It takes great wisdom and patience on the part of others to enable these tendencies to work themselves out.

It is a more difficult situation when a person really desires to confound the situation. He wants a showdown. It is a test of wills. It suggests an insincerity which is difficult, but not impossible to deal with. One thing must *not* be done. Do not react and take it as a challenge. In that case no one wins. The one doing the confronting may have the perverse satisfaction of having frustrated a divine institution if the Spiritual Assembly reacts. The assembly has nothing to gain.

A better way to handle this is to ignore the challenge of 'right or wrong' and address the question without getting drawn into an argument. If the purpose was to oppose and throw the assembly off balance, the person will be discouraged. He will probably go on his way never to bother them again.

On the other hand, if there is a spark of sincerity and the person is just responding in this childish fashion because of a temporary hurt, the approach outlined can be a balm to his soul. A healing can actually take place if the person is sincere.

There have been cases in which a person has deliberately tried to infiltrate the community to undermine it. If this is suspected, the information should immediately be given to an Auxiliary Board member or the National Spiritual Assembly and their guidance followed strictly.

For the occasional person who wishes to use the Bahá'ís for his own purposes the best thing is to treat him lovingly and openly as if he were sincere. That does not mean going along with his schemes. Consultation can take care of that. When treated as if he were sincere, he will either get discouraged and leave or the spark of faith may be ignited and grow, changing his motives.

Lying

Another type of problem which causes great difficulty is when an individual lies. This most often occurs in dealing with Bahá'í law, or the question whether specific instructions from the assembly have been carried out or not. These lies are usually told to cover up misdeeds or lack of follow-through and may be based on fear, insincerity or simply not being very deepened in the Covenant.

The essence of consultation is absolute honesty and candor. 'Abdu'l-Bahá says, *'Truthfulness is the foundation of all the virtues of mankind. Without truthfulness, progress and success in all of the worlds are impossible for a soul'* (BNE 85). Being less than honest makes the institution less effective in the work it must do.

If a person is lying to the assembly and the assembly knows it, of course it must face the individual with that. The Master gave clear instructions in this regard:

The Kingdom of God is founded upon equity and justice, and also upon mercy, compassion, and kindness to every living soul. Strive ye then with all your heart to treat compassionately all humankind – except for those who have some selfish, private motive, or some disease of the soul. Kindness cannot be shown the tyrant, the deceiver, or the thief, because, far from awakening them to the error of their ways, it maketh them to continue in their perversity as before. No matter how much kindliness ye may expend upon the liar, he will but lie the more, for he believeth you to be deceived, while ye understand him but too well, and only remain silent out of your extreme compassion. (SWAB 158)

If a person is being less than candid with the assembly but there is no real proof, there are several courses of action possible. It is all right for someone to raise the point that he does not feel that the truth is being told. This can open up a whole new range of consultation.

Another option is to be patient. What happens is that the insincerity expressed in lying sooner or later catches up with the person doing it. No purpose is served if the assembly spends a great deal of energy unmasking an individual just for the sake of making him own up to the truth.

If there is a dispute between two believers, the assembly often must come to an understanding as to what the truth is. Even then, sometimes a difference does not mean either one is lying: it may mean things are seen from different points of view.

Even a sincere person is sometimes caught in a compromising situation. In his misguided attempts to protect himself he may be tempted to lie. This often trips him up later without further effort by anyone. Even the insincere person who continues his ways will sooner or later be caught even if it seems, for a while, that he can fool the institutions. When it comes to a showdown it can be a decisive step in a person's spiritual journey. Some become stronger believers as a result even though they may have momentarily wavered. Others, caught in their own insincerity, have left the Faith or eventually had administrative rights removed, sometimes for other causes. Justice will be done.

Contentiousness

Occasionally someone brings an inexplicable and irrational form of contentiousness or anger into a Spiritual Assembly or committee. This is a negativity which is alien to attempts to establish love and harmony. It may be focused at some other member or be diffuse; it may be deliberate and malicious or it may be beyond the aggressor's control.

It really should not be too surprising that such things occur during this age of transition. The Supreme Manifestation of God has asked mankind to move forward into some ways of doing things which can seem strange and unnatural. Observing nature, animal life and man's history it seems that contention and struggle are natural. Among most groups of animals a rank order of dominance can be found; periodic power struggles erupt in an attempt to upset existing leadership roles. A look at various human enterprises suggests that the same principle applies among humans. However, Bahá'u'lláh expects modern man to sustain a relationship of love and harmony amongst people of different temperaments. This does not seem natural. Rule by domination is nature's way. The Bahá'í Writings establish consensus within divinely ordained institutions as being the new way. 'Might makes right' is the law which generally emerges when the restraining conventions of civilization are removed. Many people then become embroiled in a power struggle – an assertion of dominance. Viewed in this light, civilization itself seems like a miraculous and somewhat 'unnatural' development.

Contentiousness may well be another tool of survival which played an important role in man's evolution under more primitive conditions, a natural characteristic which found its way into the arsenal of man's lower nature.

One source of it may be a form of paranoia in which someone has little basic trust in other people, has difficulty tolerating the suspended judgment required in consultation, is rigid, especially under stress, does not understand motivation well – either his own or others' – readily misinterprets what others do and say, unintentionally creates an atmosphere of tension around himself and fails to recognize hostile overtones in his own behavior.

Or contentiousness may be intensified by or result from jealousy, a deep personal hurt, an exaggerated conflict of personality or a reversion to some former, well-entrenched, method of behavior or some other personality disorder. Regardless of the cause the results are the same: devastating!

We are reminded that *'mankind's ordered life hath been revolutionized through the agency of this unique, this wondrous System'* (GL 136). Contentiousness is among the elements of *'mankind's ordered life'* which must change under the impact of Bahá'u'lláh's new system. The Blessed Beauty has redirected differences among people, channeling them into a clash of ideas instead of a clash of power or personalities. Under the conditions of proper consultation, differences lead to enlightened consensus.

But transition from a world which has revolved around an axis of contention is not always smooth. Periodic reversions to more primitive methods of dealing with others are to be expected. Hope for mankind lies in the fact that people's mental sets do change in the incubator of the Bahá'í community; the awkward part is that an aggressor, who may be unaware of the dynamics of the power struggle being acted out, must be the one to redirect his energies. When an aggressor is slow to change, one-sided contention can erupt, with some hard-working Bahá'ís becoming unjustly maligned and attacked. In extreme situations it can become very discouraging.

Consultation itself can become misused when someone is contentious. Attention is easily misdirected to secondary issues, diverting the attention and energies of the Spiritual Assembly. Unnecessary obstacles and discouragement become placed in the path of creative projects. Enthusiasm and initiative are destroyed. Joy is drained. Creative energies are sapped and imagination is not developed. New ventures are left untried while sincere and enthusiastic believers become discouraged and shift their attention to activities not related to the Faith. A loving and accepting atmosphere is converted to one filled with tensions and inhibitions. The loss cannot be calculated, because it consists of progress not made and opportunities missed. Some Spiritual Assemblies have had their growth and development cut short by contentiousness. It is like a literal fulfillment of 'Abdu'l-Bahá's prophecy that the *'assembly be brought to naught '*: that is, the efforts of the Bahá'ís no longer produce results. Love and harmony are replaced by harsh words and turmoil, and the institution becomes temporarily derailed in its journey toward its high destiny.

'Abdu'l-Bahá spoke of three kinds of persecution. One he related to His imprisonment and chains: this He found easy to endure. The second was the lies and machinations of His enemies. Of these He said:

This form of persecution was likewise easy to bear.
But there was a third kind of persecution which brought Abdul-Baha sorrow and unhappiness, a persecution difficult to bear: the bitter words and criticism of the friends. When love was expected, hatred and jealousy was found; instead of friendship and kindness, envy and discord were manifested; instead of harmony there appeared dissension and ill-wishing; in place of assistance and appreciation, calumny, falsehood and slander. This is hard to bear. (SW IV, no. 5, p. 89)

Prolonged contention within a Bahá'í community can become like a form of persecution. He also said:

The worst enemies of the Cause are in the Cause and mention the Name of God. We need not fear the enemies on the outside for such can be easily dealt with. But the enemies who call themselves friends and who persistently violate every fundamental law of love and unity, are difficult to be dealt with in this day, for the mercy of God is great. But ere long this merciful door will be closed and such enemies will be attacked with a madness. (sw vi, no. 6, p. 45)

Under these conditions there are two temptations to be avoided. One is the impulse to fight back: to 'fight fire with fire'. That merely 'proves' erroneous accusations and increases the problem. The other temptation is to desire peace at any price, including backing off from Bahá'í activity. That, too, is fraught with danger: it is a disservice to the long-range best interests of the Cause and all concerned.

When an assembly or committee becomes a temporary battleground for contention or a power struggle, it may be a reversion or throwback to what was once an accepted, if primitive, way of challenging dominance. It may be a result of paranoia or some other malady beyond the control of the aggressor. It may be some other undesirable hold-over characteristic of the old world order. Not everyone has completed the mental transition to Bahá'u'lláh's wondrous new system.

Everything reasonable should be done to re-establish harmony; some suggestions are made in the next chapter. But if concerted efforts do not work out, let go. Learn to live with it. Everyone has his own spiritual battle. The contentious has his; one of yours is learning to live with his. Place it in perspective. Pray for him. Look for opportunities to establish harmony, but do not worry about it excessively. Concentrate on teaching. It may be best simply to leave him alone.

Until the individual himself can resolve his underlying unhealthy condition or make the transition from contentiousness to the quest for unity, further attempts to make the situation better may make it worse instead. The problem is irrational. Rational remedies do not work on irrational problems. Further attempts at peacemaking may be misunderstood and/or maliciously twisted.

In the meantime be patient. Progress can be delayed. Temporary reversals are possible. But remember: this, too, shall pass! Ultimate victory is assured as long as the faithful believers remain steadfast. This is the Cause of God! The Plan of God will triumph!

Jealousy and the Quest for Leadership

Both jealousy and the desire for leadership are types of ego problems which go beyond contentiousness. They come from extreme preoccupation with the self: the domination of the lower nature of man.

Quest for leadership

The quest for power, leadership or self-aggrandizement twists and distorts practically all activities. Everything becomes influenced by how it can be made to contribute to those ends. For instance, 'Abdu'l-Bahá says that, *'Holding to the letter of the law is many times an indication of a desire for leadership . . . when some follow merely the hard and fixed letter of the law, they deprive it* [the Revelation] *of its elastic quality – the spirit – and endeavor to convert it into a hard instrument of inflexible qualities.'* (sw vi, no. 6, pp. 43–5)

The one seeking leadership may be secretive and unwilling to share good news or ideas unless they can take on the importance of an 'announcement'. Name dropping, easy familiarity with prominent Bahá'ís and a desire for personal recognition are other symptoms of this condition.

A stand may be taken, supposedly on principle, which is way out of proportion to the issue itself. Frequently there will even be a statement such as, 'Now, there is nothing personal here . . .', or, 'This should not be taken personally, but . . .'

A project in which the person himself is involved is played up out of proportion to its real value. Equally worthy projects not involving him are apt to be minimized, brushed aside, and easily forgotten. There is an undermining, sometimes subtle and sometimes direct, of the efforts of others. It becomes an insidious and all-pervasive problem.

Subtlety is part of the elusiveness of this problem. The person himself may not be fully aware of what he is doing. He can delude himself into thinking that his only interest is to serve the Faith and that the issues about which he is speaking are really important. He may mean well. Also, one attracted to personal leadership may feel no malice toward those he is intentionally or unintentionally undermining.

Jealousy

Closely related is the individual who is jealous of those who make significant contributions to the Faith. This may be masked as concern that someone else is striving for leadership.

There are innumerable situations where jealousy can raise its head, including professional achievement, financial success, public accomplishments, even success in the teaching field. Too often when someone has special ability to attract seekers there is someone else who will criticize the methods used, the thoroughness of the teaching, or whether or not it was done with proper dignity.

There is also a common, though mistaken, notion that the Cause is the great leveler. Seeing one person do something outstanding can create feelings of frustration, anger and jealousy. Some Bahá'ís, out of a sincere, but mistaken, understanding of equality, may try to minimize the contribution made by someone else. They may try to stop the attention given the energetic one.

'Abdu'l-Bahá had a different point of view:

Envy closes the door of Bounty, and jealousy prevents one from ever attaining to the Kingdom of Abhá . . .

How regrettable: Some even use the affairs of the Cause and its activities as a means of revenge on account of some personal spite, or fancied injury, interfering with the work of another, or seeking its failure. Such only destroy their own success, did they know the truth. (sw vi, p. 44)

When one seeks leadership or is overcome with jealousy he creates an appetite for these activities which can never be satisfied. Every minor victory increases the desire for more. Sooner or later he must either have a change of heart so that he can triumph over his lower nature or his own schemes will backfire on him. In extreme cases these are the conditions which have led to Covenant-breaking.

What can be done about it when there seems to be someone so afflicted in the community? Quite a bit, really.

'Abdu'l-Bahá gave the perfect example of how to deal with these problems. Look at the way He treated Covenant-breakers *before* their activities had reached such an extreme stage that they had to be put out of the Faith. He used infinite love and patience, yet restraint. He went to great lengths to cover up their misdeeds. There is no way of knowing how many people were saved because this kind of treatment. There may have been many who had a twinge of jealousy or thirst for power at some time. But because of the wise, loving ways of the Master they were healed and remained faithful.

Consultation is an excellent tool to dispel the effects of the darkness produced by jealousy or the quest for power. Through consultation it is possible for the light of true and clear vision to flood the heart. Through consultation bickering can be set aside before its cancerous growth causes serious injury; truth can be disentangled from the web of jealousy and the darkness of power-seeking.

Consultation at times like this is at once a protection and a severe strain. Discussion can become long, laborious, sometimes heated and not very productive. Often trivia will have to be gone over and over in detail, wasting much time just to make sure a point is understood.

While difficult, that is really part of the protection: it is divine power at work. In the meantime, it is true that priceless opportunities may get lost or pushed aside. Important tasks may slip from view. Urgent matters may be delayed. But a far more important matter of preserving the integrity and the unity of the Faith – no matter how strained – is working, and that takes time. It is both a healing and a maturing process which is more important than even those items of real and grave concern which are being neglected.

It is hard discipline, but a necessary one. At work is the seasoning, the ripening, the maturing of those institutions which must deal with the full range of human potentials and foibles – from the higher to the lowest nature of man. Frustration is guaranteed. The attributes of patience and long-suffering, described by the Center of the Covenant as among the *'prime requisites'* of those who take counsel together, may well be tested to their uttermost. While the strain is great the effort is worth it. By pursuing this difficult course healing can take place, amity can flourish and the noble tasks of the assembly can once again be pursued with vigor.

In this matter there are three points to remember:

1. If the assembly gives up and lets the jealous or the power-seeker have his way, these are allowed to join the ranks of those who allowed jealousy to place them in opposition to the onward march of the Cause of God.

2. Those who do not persevere through the difficult times forfeit a precious and necessary opportunity for the maturing of themselves and the institutions. In so doing they permit human suffering to go on that much longer and be that much worse.

3. Those who turn away from the difficult times are allowing someone else to control their own spiritual well-being and destiny.

Covenant-breaking

This virulent spiritual disease is different from any other kind of problem found in the Cause. It is not the purpose of this work to discuss this odious malady, but there are three comments which should be made:

1. Neither being the cause of disunity nor disobedience to the Bahá'í laws should be confused with Covenant-breaking. Unfortunate though the other problems may be, Covenant-breaking is much worse. There is no comparison; it is a different category altogether.

2. When there is a situation of suspected violation of the Covenant it should be reported immediately to the Auxiliary Board member or assistant for protection, with all the facts. Then whatever instructions are received should be obeyed exactly and nothing more about it said to anyone.

3. Avoid known Covenant-breakers completely. This is not a matter on which to compromise. Well-intentioned though someone may be in reaching out to a Covenant-breaker, the action is filled with danger. Their literature should not be read. Any material received through the mail from one of the violators should be returned unopened and marked 'refused'. This matter should then be reported to the Auxiliary Board member or assistant or to the Spiritual Assembly.

THIRTEEN

Creating a Healing

When the voice of God spoke to mankind in this age the whole universe shook with the power of His utterance. The essence of the Message was simple and direct:

The distinguishing feature that marketh the preeminent character of this Supreme Revelation consisteth in that We have, on the one hand, blotted out from the pages of God's holy Book whatsoever hath been the Cause of strife, of malice and mischief amongst the children of men, and have, on the other, laid down the essential prerequisites of concord, of understanding, of complete and enduring unity. Well is it with them that keep My statutes. (GL 97)

It is the ultimate expression of the Cause to have unity reflected in each and every Bahá'í heart and in community life. Every effort must be made to keep strife, malice and mischief far from the community of the Greatest Name. Unity must be a constant quest; it is a great calamity when there is a stain of disunity among the followers of the King of Glory.

What should be done when disunity is present? First some precautions. It would be a mistake to try to rout out the problems by some sort of purge. An effort to get to the bottom of every issue and find out who is at fault is counter-productive. There are several things wrong with it:

1. It assumes that cleansing takes place by getting rid of the bad. Instead Bahá'u'lláh recommends changing hearts. This is a healing rather than a purge or exorcizing of evil.

2. A purge erroneously assumes two kinds of Bahá'ís. One is the good

looking for the bad to get rid of. The other is the bad, to be viewed as a source of evil. This view is contrary to the teachings.

3. We are told to get rid of the evil in our own hearts. Trying to rout it out in others requires searching for evil and negative things. Rather than solving problems, this approach causes them to grow and be prolonged because of dwelling on the unpleasant things of life.

4. A generally contentious and suspicious attitude develops rather than an atmosphere of love, harmony and peace-making. This causes a waste of precious time and resources of the divine institutions. It also can become a corruption of the divine purpose.

Except for situations of Covenant-breaking, the attempt to rout out a problem becomes a worse condition than the one it was trying to correct. It becomes the disease itself.

There are some general guidelines for dealing with the kinds of problems mentioned in the previous two chapters. There is also the assurance that by dealing with these matters improvements are made on three levels simultaneously:

1. The problem itself can be solved, reduced or accepted and endured.
2. The institutions grow, becoming stronger and more vital.
3. The individuals grow; their own spiritual lives are enriched.

As issues are faced the Spiritual Assembly will be in a better position to deal with emergencies and chaos in the future.

The key to solving problems of the very difficult nature described in the preceding chapters still lies in a common love of Bahá'u'lláh and strength in the Covenant. No other power is capable of overcoming factors which are normally so divisive. The beloved Guardian wrote, through his secretary, of this principle in a letter to Canada dated June 26, 1956:

He was very sorry to hear of the prolonged inharmony in the . . . Bahá'í community . . . Some of the . . . believers, from letters and reports received here, seem to lack a firm grounding on such matters as the Will and Testament and the deeper spiritual teachings of the Faith. Whenever the grasp of these fundamentals is weak, the friends are almost sure to pay undue attention to secondary procedures, to quibble over details, to lose themselves in personalities, and to founder in a sea of unnecessary inharmony. This has nothing to do with their devotion, their loyalty, their zeal, their eagerness to serve. It is merely a question of not having received . . . a strong enough education in the Covenant . . . (MC 58–9)

Experience as Bahá'ís, knowledge of the Faith or even theoretical knowledge of the Covenant itself are no guarantees of being free from these problems. Even some who have a good intellectual knowledge of the *Will and Testament* still may have missed the point that the main task is to establish love, unity and harmony – while allowing for differences. '. . . The members of these assemblies, on their part, must disregard utterly their own likes and dislikes, their personal interests and inclinations, and concentrate their minds upon those measures that will conduce to the welfare and happiness of the Bahá'í community and promote the common weal' (PBA 40).

The only real way to get rid of disunity is by healing and replacing the bad with the positive forces of divine love, harmony, peace and tranquility. This comes about through two specific and deliberate strategies. One involves attitudes and the other actions.

Attitudes

'*Let your vision be world-embracing, rather than confined to your own self.*' This is the advice the Blessed Beauty gave when He was speaking of that which would '*rehabilitate the fortunes of mankind*' (GL 94).

Disunity comes, in reality, from the shadows of the lower world of man. When caught in those dark recesses it is difficult to see the splendor of the larger world of Divine truth. But when one's vision is on the Divine, when one looks with a searching eye and catches a glimpse of the reality of the Supreme Manifestation of God and His stupendous Revelation, the shadows of disunity lose their importance and vanish.

Here are some thoughts that may help to keep the sincere from stumbling in the darkened path of dissension and strife.

Growth

Remember that all life is growth. When Bahá'ís are consulting together they are not only solving problems for the community, they are themselves growing. Bahá'ís are at various stages in their personal development. Not all have learned to fight their own spiritual battles. Some seem to take those battles right into Feasts and other gatherings or Spiritual Assembly meetings, making consultation more difficult.

It is important that each allow for the learning and growth not only in himself but in others. Everyone has certain areas in which he is more competent and experienced. Allowances must be made for others to be wrong, to make their mistakes and be able to learn from those experiences.

God's children

We are all children of the same Father, God. His love enfolds everyone, including those who are hard to get along with. If God loves you and at the same time has an endless outpouring of love for someone you have difficulty with, it is time to pause. You should love that person because God, who loves you, also loves him. Love him for God's sake, not his own. The Blessed Beauty said: *'If any differences arise amongst you, behold Me standing before your face, and overlook the faults of one another for My name's sake'* (GL 315).

One Bahá'í reported serving on an assembly with a woman he could hardly stand to be in the same room with. During one meeting he decided he had to overcome this problem. He focused thoughts of love toward this woman, saying over and over to himself, 'I love you, ————.' At first it gnawed at his stomach even to say it to himself. But as he tried to see the divine within her, to see her as a spiritual sister, during that meeting the hostility he had felt started to disappear. He reported that her features physically seemed to soften. Tensions seemed to evaporate. These two developed a warm affection for each other which has endured the test of time. He learned to accept her and appreciate her as she was.

The Master was asked why all who visited Him had shining countenances. He replied by saying: '. . . *in all those upon whom I look, I see only my Father's Face'* (OR 6). Most Bahá'ís can quote the Master's words about looking for the good: *'If a man has ten good qualities and one bad one, to look at the ten and forget the one; and if a man has ten bad qualities and one good one, to look at the one and forget the ten'* (BNE 83). The question is how to apply it.

One idea is to change a thought around. When a person's name is mentioned, the first thought that occurs to some people may be a disagreeable characteristic or fault. This is a common habit in today's world. When that happens pause for a moment. Remember this is a spiritual brother or sister, and replace that negative thought with a positive one by thinking or saying something good about the person. It may help to make a list of all the good qualities about someone with whom there is some difficulty.

Here is another technique which is useful when someone has said or done something offensive. Think of the higher and the lower nature of each person. If one visualizes the lower nature as a vicious guard dog within that person, problems can be handled better. If attacked, remember: it is not that 'person' attacking, it is his guard dog – his lower nature. That individual has his own spiritual struggle, part of which is keeping that dog under control. You can help by not antagonizing the beast of that lower nature.

Illumination
'Abdu'l-Bahá has referred to this world as a *'mud hut'* where *'brute traits prevail'* (SWAB 72). It is only through love, even when undeserved, that divine illumination can enter and cause the world to *'become the Abhá Paradise'*. Of this love Bahá'u'lláh said: *'The brightness of the fire of your love will no doubt fuse and unify the contending peoples and kindreds of the earth . . .'* (GL 96). Forgiveness works in this way. When one forgives, a hurt is transformed into a test. This test can then be dealt with, making healing possible and bringing greater illumination both to the individual and to all of mankind.

Interrelatedness
In His Will and Testament the Blessed Beauty left a deceptively simple method for learning to appreciate the best in everyone. He said:

We fain would hope that the people of Bahá may be guided by the blessed words: 'Say: all things are of God.' This exalted utterance is like unto water for quenching the fire of hate and enmity which smoldereth within the hearts and breasts of men. By this single utterance contending peoples and kindreds will attain the light of true unity. (TB 222)

At first glance it is hard to see how *'all things are of God'* can have such great potency. Yet there are oceans of truths in that phrase which reflection and consultation can reveal.

In order to apply this principle one must first recognize that every soul represents some facet of a gem from the mine of humanity. This blessed revelation is not just for the easy to work with or the talented; the quick-witted or slow thinkers; the disciplined or the impulsive; the competent or the tolerant; the lovable or the easily adaptable. It is for all mankind. It is the haven within which each soul can find growth, strength, and development, according to his own unique capacities.

The tricky part is to realize that the differences found in others which account for *'contending peoples and kindreds'* are also a necessary part of our own life-growth experience. 'Abdu'l-Bahá said to a pilgrim: *'Everything in life ministers to our development. Our lesson is to study and learn . . . Tests are either stumbling blocks or stepping stones, just as we make them'* (TDLA 10). This would suggest there is an inherent personal value created by someone else because he is hard to get along with. Those who cause the greatest difficulty may in fact be doing us the greatest favor. That should be taken into consideration in the attitude to be shown toward that person. *'Among the teachings of Bahá'u'lláh'*, explained 'Abdu'l-Bahá, *'is one requiring man, under all conditions and circumstances, to be forgiving, to love his enemy and to consider an ill-wisher as a well-wisher'* (BNE 8). He then goes on to warn about the hypocrisy of simply putting up with an enemy or being forbearing. Superficially that seems like a contradiction, but upon reflection there are several explanations. Here is one interesting consideration. A well-wisher desires that you develop your best qualities. When dealing with an enemy or an ill-wisher it is often necessary to call upon some inner strength and resources which you did not even know existed, or to develop some unfamiliar quality of character. It is like kneading out some gems of character from the recesses of your own soul. The result can be the same refinement of character which a well-wisher would desire.

In that tangible sense an enemy who has led you to new understandings and insights and has helped you develop your character has unwittingly acted as a true friend. This is like a gift from God and your world becomes richer as a result. This thought can quench *'the fire of hate and enmity'*.

Fault-finding

'O Son of Being! How couldst thou forget thine own faults and busy thyself with the faults of others? Who so doeth this is accursed of Me' (AHW no. 26). No one wants to be accursed of God. What could be a more terrible fate? Yet that is the result of fault-finding.

No matter what else may be said of disunity, at the basis is the human tendency to find fault with one another. This is a direct contradiction of the specific instructions from 'Abdu'l-Bahá. Being accursed follows immediately because the results of fault-finding and dwelling upon the shortcomings of one another are dissension, strife, contention, estrangement and apathy.

The proper attitude was outlined in a letter written in behalf of the Guardian concerning two believers who were having a dispute: '. . . the Guardian feels the best course of action in this matter is to ask both of the believers concerned to forgive and forget the entire matter' (LL 18). More specifically to the consequences of discord in the community he wrote:

When criticism and harsh words arise within a Bahá'í community there is no remedy except to put the past behind one, and persuade all concerned to turn over a new leaf, and for the sake of God and His Faith refrain from mentioning the subjects which have led to misunderstanding and inharmony. The more the friends argue back and forth and maintain that their point of view is right, the worse the whole situation becomes.

When we see the condition the world is in today we must surely forget these utterly insignificant internal disturbances and rush, unitedly, to the rescue of humanity. You should urge your fellow Bahá'ís to support you in a strong effort to suppress every critical thought and every harsh word, in order to let the spirit of Bahá'u'lláh flow into the entire community, and unite it in His love and in His service. (DG no. 47)

Offenses

There are two admonitions given by 'Abdu'l-Bahá which sound like different sides of the same coin. *'Let not your heart be offended with any one'*, and, *'Beware! Beware! Lest ye offend any heart'* (PF 169).

One Bahá'í makes a gesture as though to throw something over her shoulder and says, 'Praise or blame, I treat them all the same. I say "Thank you", then give them to Bahá'u'lláh and think: "Yá Bahá'u'l-Abhá!" Because everything I do is for Bahá'u'lláh, so what do I care if they don't like it. I give the blame and praise both to Bahá'u'lláh. They're His!' That precious soul harbors no grievances.

There is a basic rule of the sea which applies to interpersonal affairs and maintaining serenity in a Bahá'í community as well. Regardless who has the right-of-way, the most maneuverable ship is responsible for avoiding a collision. There are some who are easily offended, who seem primed for some type of discord. The peacemakers of the Bahá'í world are the ones who prevent the clashes, who contain disputes, who change contention into harmony, who cure disunity. Like highly maneuverable ships they not only avoid those headed for collision, but they guide others through perilous waters into a safe harbor. The Ancient Beauty must have a special love for those peacemakers – the 'maneuverable ships'. In the Persian Bayán (VII, 18) the Blessed Báb was explicit. He extolled the *'nearness to God'* of those *'who bring joy to the hearts of the believers'*. God willing, their numbers will increase.

Actions

These are lofty and noble thoughts, but how can they be applied in specific situations when a community is caught in the grips of disunity? First of all there are two clear instructions about how *not* to deal with discord:

1. Do *not* resign from committees or assemblies. Rather, tough it out. In the words of the Guardian's secretary:

> The remedy to assembly inharmony cannot be in the resignation or abstinence of any of its members. It must learn, in spite of disturbing elements, to continue to function as a whole, otherwise the whole system would become discredited through the introduction of exceptions to the rule.

> The believers, loving the Cause above all else and putting its interests first, must be ready to bear the hardships entailed, of whatever nature they may be. Only through such persistence and self-sacrifice can we ever hope to preserve, on the one hand our divine institutions intact, and on the other, force ourselves to become nobler, better instruments to serve this glorious Faith. (CC no. 36)

2. Do *not* take sides. 'The Bahá'ís must learn to forget personalities and overcome the desire – so natural in people – to take sides and fight about it' (LSA 19). There are no 'sides' in Bahá'í consultation. There are many different points of view: some may coincide, some may conflict. In searching for truth 'sides' cannot exist.

Here are some specific steps which can be taken to defeat the ugly head of contention:

1. Postpone discussion. When disunity persists in a Spiritual Assembly meeting the Master gives specific instructions about what to do:

> *The honored members of the Spiritual Assembly should exert their efforts so that no differences may occur, and if such differences do occur, they should not reach the point of causing conflict, hatred and antagonism, which lead to threats. When you notice that a stage has been reached when enmity and threats are about to occur, you should immediately postpone discussion of the subject, until wranglings, disputations, and loud talk*

vanish, and a propitious time is at hand. (CC no. 19)

2. Consult about it. While it is often best to forgive and forget about the disturbance and simply go on to other things, this does not always solve the problem. If difficulties persist it is sometimes necessary for a Spiritual Assembly to confront the issue directly, unpleasant though that may be. The utmost care, tact, patience and love are required while an attempt is being made both to find what is causing the continuous discord and to work out a solution.

3. Pray for unity. This practice has produced some astounding results. Even if only two or three believers are really aware of a problem of disunity and concerned about it, if they have an intensive prayer campaign the condition can be completely turned around.

4. Resolve differences. If estrangement centers around two individuals who seem to have a problem with each other, they could meet together (or with a third party) to try to resolve their differences.

5. Intervene. Members of a consulting group who are not part of the basic struggle should take an active rather than a passive role if the discord does not end quickly. If one member berates another, those not involved should intervene in order to try to resolve lingering issues and get on with the business in hand without hurt feelings resulting. Otherwise the one attacked feels abandoned.

6. Exercise patience and long-suffering. These are not just nice-sounding platitudes; they are real virtues which are being put to the test. This is also a time to re-examine basic motives and try to understand how actions are really perceived by others. Prayers for protection and meditating on the unwarranted accusations against the Central Figures of the Faith provide great solace.

7. Problems between people are shortened by acts of kindness. A card, a flower, a thoughtful word, gesture or phone call, an unexpected visit or gift – these all have one thing in common. They provide balm for many troubled souls; they have helped heal bad feelings between people. All it takes is the courage to take the first step.

Some people are reluctant to make a friendly gesture when they do not feel friendly. They say they do not want to act like a hypocrite. They feel funny about acting in a way they do not feel. But that is not valid. It can be an excuse, a self-righteous, almost noble-sounding refusal to take responsibility for changing the situation. Acting in a kindly way toward others improves attitudes. Hypocrisy is deliberately putting up a false front. It is a deceitful pretense of virtue for some ulterior motive. It has nothing to do with trying to make improvements, and nothing to do with attempts to change bad feelings into good or to create healing. Kind acts change feelings. So do compliments.

Complete and Enduring Unity

When the creative impulses of this age work to create healing, something magnificent happens far beyond the immediate concerns. At work is the transformation of society. It is the application of *'the Divine Elixir . . . through whose potency the crude metal of human life hath been transmuted into purest gold . . .'* (PM 54); the transferring of the principle of unity in diversity from a lofty ideal to the everyday world of life.

When there is apparent unity among Bahá'ís it is natural to think the group is becoming spiritually united and mature. That may be. It may be, however, that the Bahá'ís just happen to be compatible. Rather than achieving unity in diversity they may have a kind of unity in similarity. This can be a dangerous step toward complacency, lethargy and apathy which leads to avoidance by, rather than attraction of, those who are different. It is easy to give lip service to unity in diversity and cling to a more comfortable habit of unity without stress.

By its very nature difference produces stress. The dynamic tensions produced are the means of clearing away the rubble of prejudices and preconceived notions to the bedrock of man's spiritual existence. This can be painful.

The same range of personal characteristics that exist within the Bahá'í community are found in society as a whole. When conflicts are found in other groups it can destroy them. Wars have been started, governments toppled, great scientific or humanitarian works hampered and important business, artistic and social enterprises killed because of unresolved personality conflicts.

However, when conflicts appear within a Bahá'í setting, the power of the Covenant acts to contain the consequences. Consultation is a most valued tool in this containment. Because of the Covenant and the divine design these outbursts are actually echoes of hope. Again and again it is demonstrated that life does go on, the Cause survives and continues to strengthen and is now one episode closer to the day 'of concord, of understanding, of complete and enduring unity'. From these events come assurance and the strength to persevere in the experience and knowledge, not just the hope, of ultimate victory.

As believers use consultation to resolve immediate problems they are also taking a giant step in developing the skill of blending the diverse and sometimes antagonistic elements of mankind into a single, integrated whole. The challenge of this age is not just to take the healing Message of the Ancient Beauty to all mankind, but in so doing to love and appreciate fellow believers enough to rise above differences, overlook faults and be comfortable with each other, accepting, appreciating and even capitalizing on the differences which exist.

This challenge implies accepting the unfamiliar. It is a lesson not easily learned. When Ṭáhirih appeared without a veil at the conference of Badasht, it caused a great challenge to preconceived notions of what was 'right'. This stress was so great that 'Abdu'l-Kháliq slit his own throat – he could not face the challenge to what he thought was proper. It seems almost ludicrous to us today because that is not the way problems are handled now. But the problems of today and the methods of dealing with frustrations may seem just as ludicrous to future generations as they have difficulty coping with their own challenges.

Bahá'ís are called upon to do what is right, not just what is comfortable, familiar or easy. If unity in diversity were easy it would not have been necessary for a Prophet of God to command it. Breathing is natural and easy; it is not necessary for God to command it. The marvel of consultation, which relates the principle to the specific, makes an enormous contribution toward making the promotion of the principle of unity in diversity as natural and as easy as breathing.

That Bahá'ís find each other a test is not remarkable. Consider their varied backgrounds. That each can benefit from the experience is remarkable. Firmness in the Covenant makes that possible, as the painful metamorphosis of creating a new race of men is at work. When we see diversity at a Feast, in assemblies, at conferences, conventions and schools; when the social fabric of the Cause shows up in its many colorful and different patterns; then we will know that the healing of Bahá'u'lláh's sublime Message is at work.

In the process of establishing that *'complete and enduring unity'* advocated in the Bahá'í Writings there is one more extremely important consideration. This is to keep the objective in mind at all times and see the end in the beginning.

'Abdu'l-Bahá gave the supreme example of this. On May 1, 1912, the Master placed a stone in the ground for the dedication of the Temple Site in Wilmette, Illinois. He 'set the stone in place on behalf of all the peoples of the world. Then he [sic] said, *"The Temple is already built"* '(st 16). The dedication of that completed Temple was held forty-one years later in 1953. Yet the Divine Exemplar saw the final result clearly during the ground-breaking ceremony.

It is necessary to follow that example, to see the end in the beginning in all projects. Spiritual Assemblies must see their communities as they want them to be. They must see their task as moving the entire population of that community toward an acceptance of Bahá'u'lláh and know that has been completed in the spiritual world. Then they must gear all activities to transferring that spiritual potential to the temporal world. When they work as if the completion of each task is a reality it probably will become so.

The need now is to develop the institutions and the art of consultation. This precious gift of consultation, which the Pen of the Ancient Beauty provided, amicably resolves the very real conflicts of ideals, emotions, desires, habits, traditions, mannerisms, temperaments and personalities which normally divide people. It is guaranteed to produce welfare and well-being, illumination and understanding, awareness and certitude. It is capable of making a reality of concord and the harmonious family of man: the multicolored and splendid fabric of the future society. Achieving that result is the challenge and purpose of this age.

True, consultation sometimes slows, almost to a halt, to allow the accommodation of all conflicting personalities, but all live in this world and there is no better way for people to work together. True, much time may be wasted chasing irrelevant issues because one or more of those consulting does not seem connected with what is going on, but there is no better way to promote harmony. True, it would be simpler to go about one's business without worrying about people who differ so vastly, but isolation does not work in this complex and interrelated world. Ignoring problems does not make them go away.

True, there are more 'efficient' ways to operate, but there is no more enduring way, no matter how long it takes, no matter how many times the same lessons must be learned and relearned.

Some problems of discord can be solved. Solve them. Some cannot; they must be endured. They will pass. The love of Bahá'u'lláh is the glue which holds dissimilar people together until happier times come. In the meantime unity in diversity – the challenge of this age – nurtured through consultation, slowly ripens to maturity and, phoenix-like, a new world emerges from the ashes of contention.

FOURTEEN

Reflections On Consultation

The gift of consultation is so filled with awesome possibilities that it is impossible to consider them all. It seems appropriate, however, to pause and reflect upon a few aspects of a general nature.

Ebb and Flow

Change is possibly the most predictable thing there is in life. Nothing remains the same. Nothing remains static. In the medium obligatory prayer, Bahá'u'lláh speaks of the *'changes and chances of life'*. In *The Hidden Words* He tells us that we should *'Be not troubled in poverty nor confident in riches, for poverty is followed by riches, and riches are followed by poverty'* (PHW no. 51). He also stated that *'both shall pass away and be no more'* (AHW no. 52). However one chooses to define 'wealth' or 'poverty' there is a suggestion of changing events. Further, on the same theme, He said, *'Be generous in your days of plenty, and patient in the hour of loss. Adversity is followed by success and rejoicings follow woe'* (TB 138).

The beloved Guardian informed us that the history of the Faith of Bahá'u'lláh 'may be said to resolve itself into a series of pulsations, of altering crises and triumphs . . .' (GPB 409).

Change and the cycles of events are also seen in the lapping of water during its ebb and flow. One of the most refreshing experiences of life is to watch the shore of a large body of water. There are sensuous delights of sight, sound, feeling and smell in these rhythmic pulsations which can bring a balm to a troubled heart – a unique tranquility. It seems to capture the essence of the rhythms in all aspects of life. The root meaning of the word 'flow' is to rinse or to wash. The energetic forward surge of the flow, followed by the relaxing retreat of the ebb, has a wonderful effect. The one shows strength – sometimes gentle, sometimes fierce – the other shows the condition of repose. Neither is complete without the other. Both are part of that dynamic unity that allows the whole creation to function in matched cycles of rhythmic perfection.

During the seemingly placid ebb there is much activity beneath the surface. There may be undertows or cross-currents of awesome violence, creating great danger. This is part of the natural rhythm. It is part of the healing and cleansing process of life.

Examples of cycles of rhythms are endless: night, day, the tides, the seasons, the phases of the moon. From the moment of conception there is growth in each human life. This growth is not steady but speeds up and slows down in spurts and starts. In adults there are patterned changes in mood, alertness and peak efficiency. Stress, such as an emergency situation or an exciting opportunity, can alter the patterns of the rhythms, but they cannot be eliminated. This is the pattern of life, the pattern of development.

Consultation, too, has its ebb and flow. This is true during any given meeting, over the course of a year and even over the years. There will be times in any group when consultation will flow with awesome smoothness, when there is peak performance. There may be other times when that same group finds consultation bogged down. This need not cause alarm or despair – it may be a natural ebbing in the life of the consulting body. Even where there seems to be a major deterioration in consultation the ebb can and does end.

It is necessary to understand this ebb and flow so as not to become too proud of accomplishments nor discouraged by poor results. The Writings admonish us to treat blame and praise the same. One possible understanding of this is that whatever it is that brings praise or blame may merely be extreme points of the same cycle. They are linked together, neither possible without the other.

As the institutions of this majestic Cause develop we should remember that growth will be cyclical rather than steady. However, there can be no complacency. There is a major difference between the ebb and flow of the surging sea and changes in the fortunes of man. Implicit in the ebb of the sea is the gathering of forces and momentum for the following flow.

A low point in the development of consultation or the growth of the Cause is the basis for a future burst forward only to the degree that the hearts of the believers are channels for triumph. The surge forward will not happen by itself. It will happen because lovers of Bahá'u'lláh became willing instruments, allowing the mysterious forces of this glorious Cause to surge through them. Then renewed bursts forward will fulfill the potential in the ebb, leading the Faith of Bahá'u'lláh, in the words of the Guardian, 'ever nearer to its divinely appointed destiny' (GPB 409).

Consultation and the Formative Age

The Beloved Guardian divided the Dispensation of Bahá'u'lláh into three distinct ages. The first was named the Heroic Age (it was also called the Apostolic or Iron Age). It began with the declaration of the Báb on May 23, 1844, and ended with the Ascension of 'Abdu'l-Bahá on November 28, 1921. The second stage, the Formative Age, began at that time, and will be followed by the Golden Age to begin some time in the future. Each of these ages has its own contributions to make to the evolution of the Cause; each has its distinctive characteristics.

This is the Formative Age. As its name implies, it is the time when the distinguishing features of the new world develop and assume their proper form. This is when the mighty institutions of the Cause must be reared and become effectively functioning. This is when the foundations of Bahá'í society are laid. This is the time of the first stirrings of the new world civilization. It is a time of pulsation, of uncertainty and of stress; a time of crisis and victory; a time of disappointment and triumph; a time for sailing in the uncharted seas; a time of new and ever-changing challenges.

It has also been referred to as the age of frustration. There are glimpses of the promises of the new day to come but most of the work must be done amidst the debris and rubble of the old civilization as it totters on the brink of final collapse.

The Guardian brilliantly described the condition of the world at this stage:

What we witness at the present time . . . is the adolescent age in the slow and painful evolution of humanity . . . The tumult of this stage of transition is characteristic of the impetuosity and irrational instincts of youth, its follies, its prodigality, its pride, its self-assurance, its rebelliousness, and contempt of discipline. (PDC 121)

Bahá'ís working in the midst of this condition of confusion find endless frustrations. There is frustration because it is so clear that the laws, the principles and the processes inaugurated by the Pen of Bahá'u'lláh can so easily solve the problems, large and small, afflicting the world of today. Yet the world stumbles along ignoring these solutions. It is the age of frustration because the priceless gift of this new Revelation is placed before a heedless, uncaring and veiled society. And it is the Bahá'ís, largely unskilled for so awesome a task, who have been given the responsibility of nurturing this new gift. This is the age of frustration during which processes and tools of enormous power are used by Bahá'ís. The believers of these perilous times use these gifts even though they do not understand clearly the supreme nature of their task nor what to do with these potent instruments. It is the age of frustration because the needs are so great and the resources so limited.

Within this milieu strength and energies are being gathered and focused to establish the foundation of the new world civilization. A fascinating feature of this process is that several levels of development are at work simultaneously. Each level has its own pattern of ebb and flow, of peak performance and apparent reversals.

The purpose of every human being on the face of the planet is to know and worship God. The collective responsibility of mankind is to carry forward an ever-advancing civilization. The challenge of the Formative Age is to build the tools for the erection of the new civilization. The Blessed Beauty has provided the means by which all three things happen at the same time.

Spiritual fulfillment comes when individuals devote energies to the forward movement of the Cause. Individual salvation brought by the Ancient Beauty requires nothing less than the energetic spread of the Faith and development of those agencies which will take care of all mankind. An irony of this age is that personal salvation comes from forgetfulness of self and submerging one's self into the work of collective salvation.

The primary tool for this work is consultation. It is also one of the fundamental elements in the building of the divine edifice for the future. At this stage of development, consultation is crude and elementary. Nonetheless, it is the most appropriate tool for the task. This tool, necessary both for today and the future, is being honed, refined and developed while the process is going on. As a problem arises, an aspect of the divine scheme capable of addressing it is developed. The needs of the day trigger the required development. All the solutions potentially lie within the framework already established.

This generation stands too close to the work being done to have a true appreciation of the marvel which is being performed. Future generations will look back in awe at what was accomplished during these difficult times. They will know that the gift of the new world civilization was built by blood, sweat, tears, frustration and toil of ordinary believers during a turbulent period in history.

These times bring a unique joy. It is not the joy of having plans work easily and smoothly; it is the joy of hard-won and sometimes small victories purchased by mighty effort. A joy that comes from the conviction that no matter what the trials, no matter what the cost, it is a divine work, and that the work is going forward despite minor setbacks. Furthermore, it is the only work guaranteed to provide security for future generations; to eliminate the threat of war and to prepare the way for the Golden Age anticipated by all religions of the past.

Consultation in local communities, in assemblies, in families, or among friends is the key to the release of these joys and the fulfillment of the promises made by the Báb that this religion would *'become universal and include all the people of the world'* (LL 11).

The Legacy

In *Some Answered Questions* the Master compares the development of man as a species to the development of an embryo. He states that the various stages the embryo goes through are the same as the stages that mankind went through (SAQ 177-9).

The comparison is fascinating, and it is also interesting to apply this analogy to the present stage in the Formative Age of the World Order of Bahá'u'lláh. The Guardian often referred to the embryonic world order. Just as it is impossible to tell what the man will look like when looking at the infant, let alone the embryo, so too it is impossible to tell, in detail, the nature of the institutions and the form consultation will take in the future.

But the embryo must be protected, for if it is damaged, the adult it will eventually become may be affected. Some examples in nature are the experiments made on butterflies: caterpillars have been cut, and their wounds allowed to heal. There is no apparent scar as they enter the cocoon stage. Only when the butterfly comes out of the cocoon can marks be found which represent the cuts received earlier. This illustrates what happens when there is damage at some phase of development.

These features in the life of the individual are similar to what happens in the life of mankind. The civilization of the future will function with the marvelous tool of consultation which has been provided to meet the changing needs of this and future generations.

Bahá'ís in the Formative Age of the Faith have been entrusted with the development of this mechanism which will be the basis of all future human enterprises. It is vital that during this crucial period no distortions or corruptions stain the fundamentals of the consultative process. This is ensured by keeping eyes fixed on the Creative Word at all times. Any deviation from this, any introduction of man-made systems, may produce an effect similar to that of the wound to the caterpillar. Constant use of and reference to the Word of God maintains the purity of the divine process.

A further responsibility is the transmission of the precious gift of consultation to the next generation. The more vigorously the consultative process is developed in all aspects of life, the easier and the more natural that transmission will be. That training starts in the home and is further developed in the life of the community.

The successful survival, protection and transmission of consultation are possible through the strength of the Covenant. There is no other power on earth capable of performing such an overwhelming feat. This relationship with the Covenant is the source of life to individual souls. It is also the strength of the community, the promise of the future and the only thing that permits the Bahá'ís of today to transmit the legacy of consultation intact and undefiled to future generations.

Epilogue

On January 12, 1922, the beloved Guardian, Shoghi Effendi, wrote one of his first messages to the Bahá'ís of North America. It was just six weeks after 'Abdu'l-Bahá's ascension and only two weeks after Shoghi Effendi had received the staggering news that he was the Guardian of the infant Cause of God.

In touching and tender terms he wrote:

At this early hour when the morning light is just breaking upon the Holy Land, whilst the gloom of the dear Master's bereavement is still hanging thick upon the hearts, I feel as if my soul turns in yearning love and full of hope to that great company of His loved ones across the seas, who now share with us all the agonies of His separation. (BA 15)

This gentle note sounded the beginning of the Formative Age of the Faith. Throughout His ministry the Guardian slowly and steadily opened the eyes of the believers to the stupendous potential within this Cause. In 1934 he reminded one and all: 'Let no one, while this System is still in its infancy, misconceive its character, belittle its significance or misrepresent its purpose' (WOB 156).

In his letter bearing the title 'The Unfoldment of World Civilization', the Guardian proclaimed:

Unification of the whole of mankind is the hall-mark of the stage which human society is now approaching. Unity of family, of tribe, of city-state and nation have been successfully attempted and fully established. World unity is the goal towards which a harassed humanity is striving. Nation-building has come to an end. The anarchy inherent in state sovereignty is moving towards a climax. A world, growing to maturity must abandon this fetish, recognize the oneness and wholeness of human relationships, and establish once for all the machinery that can best incarnate this fundamental principle of its life. (WOB 202)

He then proceeded to list over thirty of the principles of the new world civilization. In that same letter he spoke of the two forces at work in the world.

The constructive process stands associated with the nascent Faith of Bahá'u'lláh, and is the harbinger of the New World Order that Faith must erelong establish. The destructive forces that characterize the other should be identified with a civilization that has refused to answer to the expectation of a new age, and is consequently falling into chaos and decline. (WOB 170)

As we cast our eyes on the vision of the future world civilization described by Bahá'u'lláh the picture looks very bright indeed. When we focus attention on the trials presently engulfing all mankind the future looks bleak and uncertain. Perspective can be maintained when one realizes where we are in history, that there are cycles of ebb and flow, challenge and victory, and that within the community of the Greatest Name there is a legacy for handling both today's problems and establishing the dreamed-of future world civilization.

Bahá'ís are extremely fortunate to have three special gifts to sustain them in this time of peril.

1. First and foremost is the vision of the future given by the Writings. No matter how dark the immediate horizons, the fortunes of mankind in the distant future are unspeakably glorious. From the outset of this beloved Cause there has been a unique promise. The blessed Báb, in His address to the Letters of the Living, outlined the life each must lead and the duties to be performed. He concluded with these stirring words: *'Arise in His name, put your trust wholly in Him, and be assured of ultimate victory'* (DB 94).

This assurance was kept in the hearts of those holy souls and was their strength in all manner of trials and difficulties. Throughout the decades of the onward march of this glorious Cause the assurance of ultimate victory has been blazoned in the hearts of its lovers, giving them courage to withstand all tests. Knowing with certainty that this victory will be achieved is as sure a source of strength today as it was in the days of Shaykh Tabarsí and it will continue to be so tomorrow.

2. With the love of Bahá'u'lláh and the protection of His Covenant

there is a personal confidence, serenity and composure that enables everyone to withstand the trials and tribulations which may confront them. This is true both in one's personal life and in the life of the Cause. In one of His prayers Bahá'u'lláh gives the assurance that, *'Armed with the power of Thy name nothing can ever hurt me, and with Thy love in my heart all the world's afflictions can in no wise alarm me'* (PM 208). This has been put to the test and proven.

3. The crumbling caused by the relentless rolling up of the old world order spews rubble, devastation and chaos on every side. This becomes a part of everyday life. The urgency of any given day in many parts of the world is reduced to basic survival – food, shelter, protection. During this tumultuous transition it is difficult to keep our vision focused on the glories of a distant future. The urgency, the crises of today, the empty stomachs, must be dealt with. Bahá'u'lláh has said: *'O ye peoples of the world! Know, verily, that an unforeseen calamity is following you . . .'* (GL 209).

Unforeseen means unforeseen: that while even more troublesome times ahead are certain, their nature is unknown. There is no way to prepare adequately for a future emergency the nature of which is completely unknown. However, the Blessed Beauty in His unending providence gave the magnificent tool of consultation. With this tool the best can be made of any situation, no matter how hopeless it may appear nor how novel it seems. With this tool the limited resources available can be used to their best advantage. The group of Bahá'ís which learns, through consultation, to deal with routine problems – large and small – of community life, develops the basic tool of survival required for the tortuous days ahead. Thus armed, believers can make the best of the unpredictable and regrettable circumstances which confront them. They will have learned to face difficult questions and make hard decisions while maintaining unity and a sense of purpose. That is the best preparation there is for the unpredictable future.

Now, as we contemplate the future and look beyond the dark shadows cast upon our feet, some of the distinguishing features of the future World Order create a vivid and striking silouette. While many of the essential features of that vision are still embryonic some elements have passed beyond that. They have been born and appear in their early stages.

The Universal House of Justice is established. Divine Law has been proclaimed. The essential institutions have been initiated. Fundamental features of Bahá'í society have been delineated. Calamities and triumphs have forged a strong sense of community. Daily events continue to weave the fine fabric of an exquisite Bahá'í society. Bahá'í principles are increasingly put to work in the practical arena of everyday life.

Out of the rubble of the rotting old world there is fresh evidence of the growth, the vitality, the virility of the new civilization being spread out in its stead. The growing strength of the Bahá'í communities; the increasing recognition by public officials – both friends and foes – of the presence and influence of the Cause; the spread of the Faith to the far corners of the globe, to every land and clime; the allegiance of avowed supporters of the varied nations, tribes and strata of human society; the rising number of believers, centers and Spiritual Assemblies; the expanding numbers of incorporated and vigorously functioning assemblies; the increase of its prestige and properties attest the rapid growth, stability and endurance of the Cause of God in this day.

A cursory glance at the results of the past century-and-a-half, of the past half-century, or the past decade, or indeed the past year, inspires fresh hope for the future development of this great Cause. It is with renewed confidence, born of demonstrable evidence of progress, that we can gaze beyond the dark shadows before us into the brilliant future and, like the heroes, saints, martyrs, exemplary believers and ordinary lovers of the Blessed Beauty from ages past, we, too, can be *'assured of ultimate victory'*.

As the beloved Guardian so eloquently stated,

Ours, dearly-beloved co-workers, is the paramount duty to continue, with undimmed vision and unabated zeal, to assist in the final erection of that edifice the foundations of which Bahá'u'lláh has laid in our hearts, to derive added hope and strength from the general trend of recent events, however dark their immediate effects, and to pray with unremitting fervor that He may hasten the approach of the realization of that Wondrous Vision which constitutes the brightest emanation of His Mind and the fairest fruit of the fairest civilization the world has yet seen. (WOB 48)

Key to References

ABL   *'Abdu'l-Bahá in London.* London, Bahá'í Publishing Trust, 1982.

ADJ   *The Advent of Divine Justice,* Shoghi Effendi. Wilmette, Bahá'í Publishing Trust, 1956.

AHW   see HW.

BA   *Bahá'í Administration,* letters from Shoghi Effendi. Wilmette, Bahá'í Publishing Trust, 1960.

BMFL   *Bahá'í Marriage and Family Life,* a compilation, National Spiritual Assembly of the Bahá'ís of Canada. Wilmette, Bahá'í Publishing Trust, 1983.

BM, NDF   *Bahá'í Meetings, The Nineteen Day Feast,* a compilation. Wilmette, Bahá'í Publishing Trust, 1976.

BNE   *Bahá'u'lláh and the New Era,* J. E. Esslemont. Wilmette, Bahá'í Publishing Trust, 1980.

BWF   *Bahá'í World Faith,* a compilation. Wilmette, Bahá'í Publishing Trust, 1956.

CB   *The Covenant of Bahá'u'lláh,* a compilation. London, Bahá'í Publishing Trust, 1963.

CBL   *Centers of Bahá'í Learning,* a compilation. Wilmette, Bahá'í Publishing Trust, 1980.

CC   *Consultation: A Compilation,* The Universal House of Justice. Wilmette, Bahá'í Publishing Trust, 1980.

DAL   *The Divine Art of Living,* a compilation, Mabel Hyde Paine. Wilmette, Bahá'í Publishing Trust, 1944.

DB   *The Dawn-Breakers, Nabíl's Narrative.* New York, Bahá'í Publishing Committee, 1932.

official Bahá'í agencies. RP Oxford, George Ronald, 1978.

SWAB   *Selections from the Writings of 'Abdu'l-Bahá.* Haifa, Bahá'í World Centre, 1978.

SWB   *Selections from the Writings of the Báb.* Haifa, Bahá'í World Centre, 1978,

TB   *Tablets of Bahá'u'lláh Revealed after the Kitáb-i-Aqdas.* Haifa, Bahá'í World Centre, 1978.

TDLA   *Ten Days in the Light of 'Akká,* Julia M. Grundy. RP Wilmette, Bahá'í Publishing Trust, 1979.

TDP   *Tablets of the Divine Plan,* 'Abdu'l-Bahá. Wilmette, Bahá'í Publishing Trust, 1977.

UD   *Unfolding Destiny, the Messages from the Guardian of the Bahá'í Faith to the Bahá'í Community of the British Isles.* London, Bahá'í Publishing Trust, 1981.

USBN   *Bahá'í News.* A publication of the National Spiritual Assembly of the Bahá'ís of the United States.

USBP   *Bahá'í Prayers.* Wilmette, Bahá'í Publishing Trust, 1982.

V   *Vignettes from the Life of 'Abdu'l-Bahá,* Annamarie Honnold. Oxford, George Ronald, 1982.

WG   *Wellspring of Guidance,* messages from the Universal House of Justice 1963–1968. Wilmette, Bahá'í Publishing Trust, 1969.

WO   *World Order,* a magazine. Published by the National Spiritual Assembly of the Bahá'ís of the United States.

WOB   *The World Order of Bahá'u'lláh,* letters from Shoghi Effendi. Wilmette, Bahá'í Publishing Trust, 1944.

DG   *Directives from the Guardian.* New Delhi, Bahá'í Publishing Trust, 1973.

DND   *Dawn of a New Day, Messages to India 1923–1957,* Shoghi Effendi. New Delhi, Bahá'í Publishing Trust, 1973.

GL   *Gleanings from the Writings of Bahá'u'lláh.* Wilmette, Bahá'í Publishing Trust, 1951.

GPB   *God Passes By,* Shoghi Effendi. Wilmette, Bahá'í Publishing Trust, 1950.

HE   *High Endeavours, Messages to Alaska,* Shoghi Effendi. National Spiritual Assembly of the Bahá'ís of Alaska, 1976.

HW   *The Hidden Words,* Bahá'u'lláh. Wilmette, Bahá'í Publishing Trust, 1963.

IT   *The Individual and Teaching,* a compilation. Wilmette, Bahá'í Publishing Trust, 1977.

JWTA   *Japan Will Turn Ablaze,* letters from 'Abdu'l-Bahá and Shoghi Effendi. Japan, Bahá'í Publishing Trust, 1974.

KI   *Kitáb-i-Íqán. The Book of Certitude,* Bahá'u'lláh. Wilmette, Bahá'í Publishing Committee, 1951.

LBC   *Life Blood of the Cause,* a compilation, The Universal House of Justice. London, Bahá'í Publishing Trust, 1971.

LG   *Lights of Guidance: A Bahá'í Reference File,* Helen Hornby. New Delhi, Bahá'í Publishing Trust, 1983.

LGANZ   *Letters from the Guardian to Australia and New Zealand, 1923–1957.* National Spiritual Assembly of the Bahá'ís of Australia, 1970.

LL   *Living the Life,* a compilation. London, Bahá'í Publishing Trust, 1974.

LSA   *The Local Spiritual Assembly,* a compilation, The Universal House of Justice. Wilmette, Bahá'í Publishing Trust, 1970.

MC   *Messages to Canada,* Shoghi Effendi. National Spiritual Assembly of the Bahá'ís of Canada, 1965.

MNF   'Marriage and the Nuclear Family: A Bahá'í Perspective', Khalil A. Khavari, *Bahá'í Studies Notebook,* Vol. III, Nos. 1 & 2, March 1983. Association for Bahá'í Studies, Ottawa, 1983.

MUHJ   *Messages from the Universal House of Justice, 1968–1973.*
            Wilmette, Bahá'í Publishing Trust, 1976.

NSA   *The National Spiritual Assembly,* a compilation, The
            Universal House of Justice. Wilmette, Illinois, 1972.

OR   *The Oriental Rose or the Teachings of Abdul Baha,* Mary
            Hanford Ford. New York, Broadway Publishing Co.,
            1910.

PBA   *Principles of Bahá'í Administration,* a compilation.
            London, Bahá'í Publishing Trust, 1950.

PDC   *The Promised Day Is Come,* Shoghi Effendi. Wilmette,
            Bahá'í Publishing Trust, 1961.

PF   *Portals to Freedom,* Howard Colby Ives. Oxford, George
            Ronald, 1976.

PM   *Prayers and Meditations by Bahá'u'lláh.* Wilmette, Bahá'í
            Publishing Committee, 1954.

PP   *The Priceless Pearl,* Rúḥíyyih Rabbani. London, Bahá'í
            Publishing Trust, 1969.

PT   *Paris Talks,* 'Abdu'l-Bahá. London, Bahá'í Publishing
            Trust, 1951.

PHW   see HW.

PUP   *The Promulgation of Universal Peace,* 'Abdu'l-Bahá. Wil-
            mette, Bahá'í Publishing Trust, 2nd edn. 1982.

RBii   *The Revelation of Bahá'u'lláh, Adrianople 1863–1868,*
            Adib Taherzadeh. Oxford, George Ronald, 1977.

SAQ   *Some Answered Questions,* 'Abdu'l-Bahá. Wilmette,
            Bahá'í Publishing Trust, 1981.

SCK   *Selection and Codification of the Laws and Ordinances of
            the Kitáb-i-Aqdas.* Haifa, Bahá'í World Centre, 1973.

SF   *Spiritual Foundations: Prayer, Meditation and the Devo-
            tional Attitude,* a compilation, The Universal House of
            Justice. Wilmette, Bahá'í Publishing Trust, 1980.

SML   *A Special Measure of Love,* a compilation. Wilmette, Bahá'í
            Publishing Trust, 1974.

ST   *The Spell of the Temple,* Allen Boyer McDaniel. New
            York, Vantage Press, 1953.

SW   *Star of the West,* the Bahá'í Magazine, published from 1910
            to 1933 from Chicago and Washington, DC by